Common Cents

Paul C. Haughey

"Common Cents," by Paul C. Haughey.
ISBN 978-1-62137-882-2 (softcover), 978-1-62137-884-6 (eBook), 978-1-62137-883-9 (hardcover).

Library of Congress Number on file with publisher.

Table of Contents

Acknowledgments

I would like to thank the illustrators for the cartoon drawings: Jonathan Brown, Austen Redinger and Guadalupe Rivas. I would also like to thank my reviewers Richard Leland, Dan O'Daly, Philip Haughey and Dave Sloane. Finally, I want to thank my wife Denise Spencer for her support and pithy comments.

*Perhaps the sentiments contained in the following pages, are not **yet** sufficiently fashionable to procure them general favor; a long habit of not thinking a thing **wrong**, gives it a superficial appearance of being **right**, and raises at first a formidable outcry in defense of custom.*
Common Sense, Thomas Paine, 1st sentence (1776)

Introduction

IN THE UNITED STATES we disagree on many things, but we agree on two things that would appear contradictory. (1) We revere our Constitution. (2) The political system has stopped working. The main value of politics is providing material for comedians. Our government has deteriorated into extreme partisanship and gridlock, unable to do anything significant. This has been getting worse for decades. Meanwhile, government debt has skyrocketed and the disparity between rich and poor is at an all-time high. We are losing the engine of our consumer economy– the middle class. It's like a self-driving car that has been hacked and is taking us over a cliff.

Many citizens don't bother to vote anymore (60% don't vote in midterm elections, 40% don't vote in presidential elections). Many think their votes don't count, and as I will show, they are right. Voters are angry, with a Tea Party revolt among Republicans, and a socialist revolt by Bernie Sanders supporters. Principled politicians are forced out of office or are quitting, and good people won't run. Voters are supporting the unconventional Donald Trump, hoping – yet again – that an outsider will change Washington. But sending more radical candidates and outsiders to Washington will not solve the problem – they will fail. It is like asking elite Navy Seals to mount an open field charge against enemy machine guns in WWI– they would get slaughtered just like other soldiers before them. We don't need better soldiers; we need to change the system.

Most people focus on the presidential race, but it is Congress that makes the laws. Congress is the referee for our economy, and the referee has been bought off. Over the years, special interests (corporations, unions & other organized groups) have lobbied for government laws and regulations that have tilted the economy to their advantage at the expense of the common citizen. The rigged

1

favors to special interests are destroying the middle class engine of our consumer-based economy. This threatens your pocketbook and the position of the United States in the world. It also threatens the special interests themselves, which need people to be able to buy their products, or pay their dues. The stakes couldn't be higher.

If the rules for boxing required the challenger to wear handcuffs, what would be the result? Similarly, we can't put good people in a government system funded by special interests and expect them to succeed without becoming beholden to special interests. The solution isn't stronger boxers – it's removing the handcuffs.

Special interests are good and necessary organizations and they lobby for appropriate causes. Corporations drive our economy and provide jobs and investments for us. Unions provide living wages. Environmental groups protect our environment and other organized groups perform other necessary functions. However, under our adversarial political and economic system, they are incentivized to take as much advantage as the system (that's us) allows.

Many of us are members of special interests, but most of us would not want our special interest to take advantage of the rest of the country. Members of AARP would be mortified to see the costs of their benefits paid for by their children and grandchildren through debt, leaving no money for similar benefits for their children and grandchildren. While NRA members want their guns, 75% of the members are in favor of background checks to prevent purchase by criminals and the mentally ill.[1] Most environmentalists want to preserve virgin forests, not have environmental laws used to drive up the costs of development in urban neighborhoods, which drives up housing costs for their kids.[2] Instead of a rising tide lifting all boats, we have thousands of siphoning leaks draining the ocean for all of us. Of course, *you* don't need to give up the unjust benefits of your special interest– it is only *your neighbor*'s special interests that are taking unfair advantage.

The Constitutional checks and balances, providing divided government, theoretically allow everyone to be heard, and forces opposing views to compromise. But Congress and the political parties have distorted the system over time so that only special interests have a seat at the table, each getting what it wants, while the rest of us foot the bill. The "balances" of the "checks and balances" have been lost in the last few decades, replaced by a proliferation of checks that has led to gridlock.

There are common sense solutions to most of our problems that the vast majority of Americans would agree on. But our system of divided government requires compromise to act on these. The Constitution itself was a series of compromises, and is structured to divide power and force compromise. Refusal to compromise is not principled– it is rejecting the Founders vision for our government as embodied in the Constitution. Compromise has become increasingly rare, and we need to address the factors making compromise difficult. We need to understand the underlying structural problems, and address them, before we can make any significant progress on substantive issues. Once the structural problems are understood, the solutions become obvious. To understand the problems with our political system, you don't need to be a political scientist – you just need some common sense and know how to follow the money.

So what has gone wrong? We need to start at the beginning to understand.

Summary of U.S. Constitution provisions to avoid concentration of power

During the revolutionary war, the Continental Congress adopted the first U.S. constitution, the Articles of Confederation,

4

in 1777. It was ratified by all the states in 1781. Because the states didn't want to give up power, the federal government had very little power, and thus couldn't do much (rumor has it that the Tea Party is dusting off the Articles of Confederation). Among its provisions was a single congress (no house & senate), funding provided by the states, and a requirement that all the states to agree to any amendment. The "Federalists" wanted a stronger national government, while the "Anti-Federalists" wanted the states to be stronger. After 6 years there was general agreement that it wasn't working well, so the Constitutional Convention was convened in the summer of 1787 to revise the Articles of Confederation. Instead, after some delegates walked out, they wrote a new document: our Constitution. Many states balked at approving it until 10 amendments were added, the Bill of Rights.

Ours was the first modern democratic republic, and thus the Constitution was literally an experiment. It was shorter than subsequent constitutions of other countries, leaving details to be developed by Congress (Hmmm– perhaps not a good idea?). We all know its basic structure– 3 branches of government, the Congress, President (executive branch) and the judiciary.

Congress was given both a House and a Senate, instead of being a single body.[3] The large states proposed two chambers, both elected based on population, while the small states proposed a single body with each state having equal representation, as in the failed Articles of Confederation. The convention deadlocked on this issue until the Connecticut Compromise that enabled the Constitution to get the votes it needed. The compromise was to provide each state equal representation in the Senate, with representation based on population in the House. The Senate thus gave the minority in the less populated states the ability to block the will of the majority. The differences in population between states have grown since then. Today, 18% of the population can control a majority in the Senate (the 26 least populated states).[4]

The three branches of government were to check and balance each other to avoid the concentration of power. The Founders main fear was that once in power, those elected wouldn't want to relinquish power, and would convert the United States into a

5

dictatorship or establish a king. This was a legitimate fear, and has happened to a number of subsequent democracies.[5] In Latin America, constitutions often get suspended or amended to remove any limits on terms, and re-election is assured through media take-overs and voting fraud.

The Founders were not just afraid of a new king or dictatorship, they were also afraid of democracy, in particular of tyranny by the majority. The whole point of the Bill or Rights was to protect the minority from the majority. Direct democracy is mob rule, and mobs can be enflamed by demagogues who appeal to people's worst instincts. In such a system, the government tends to pander to the interests of the majority. This can be destructive– for example, a majority of poor people could enact confiscatory taxes on businesses and the rich. The far left would love this, but it would drive the economy into the ground, as in Venezuela. Or worse, in Iraq, for example, it means the majority Shia can take bloodthirsty revenge on the minority Sunni's. The Founders purposefully designed our system to avoid direct democracy.[6] As a result, we were given a representative democracy, or republic, under our Constitution– not a pure democracy.

The Founders did all they could to isolate the government from the voters. Senators were originally elected by state legislatures, not popular vote. The Founders wanted senators insulated from pressure from the populace. The House was elected directly by voters in each state, but the states set the rules for who could vote, with most of the states requiring that voters pay taxes and/or own a specified amount of property (along with being male, and not black).

The election of the president and vice president by electors (the "electoral college") was another compromise at the Constitutional Convention. The number of electors corresponded to the number of senators and representatives, and thus was another outgrowth of the tension between the big and small states.

The original proposal was to have the president elected by Congress, similar to the parliamentary systems adopted by most democracies subsequent to ours. That would have spared us a lot of the grief we have today with Congress and the President in different parties trying to thwart each other instead of working together! Direct election of the president by popular vote was rejected, and instead each state would select "electors" who would then use their independent judgment to vote for the president. The Constitution does not require the selection of electors by popular vote, and originally state legislatures selected electors. A popular vote was a practice widely adopted many years later in 1824. It was anticipated that most of the time there would be no clear majority because most states' electors would choose president and vice-president candidates from their own state. That is why the Constitution requires at least one candidate from another state.[7] The Constitution provides that, when there isn't a majority, the House of Representatives would decide from the 3 top candidates.[8] In essence, the electors were to provide candidates to the House.[9] The Founders' wariness about direct democracy should give us pause when we hear proposals for more direct democracy as a solution to our problems.

This designed separate election of the president and the two houses of Congress may avoid tyranny, but at a high price. It is the major overriding feature of our Constitution that enables gridlock and makes it difficult to govern, leading to a host of problems discussed below. It is hard to see this changing, and thus we must confront and deal with the consequences.

I. What Isn't In The Constitution

THE WORKABILITY OF THE CONSTITUTION depends on Congress implementing reasonable rules. The details left out of the Constitution have enabled a lot of mischief by Congress. Many people would be surprised at how much of our system isn't in the Constitution, and how much is recent.

Winner-take-all elections.
The current "winner-take-all" practice of all the votes of a state going to whomever wins a majority of votes in that state is not in the Constitution. It can be changed by each state's legislature. "Winner-take-all" means that the winner of 50.1% of the vote gets 100% of that state's electoral votes (sort of like our economy, except the winners are the top 1%). The winner-take-all system also applies to each congressional district in most states as well. The alternative is proportional representation where the minority can elect a minority of the representatives, instead of none. Most of the original 13 states did not have a winner-take-all system, and instead had multi-member districts,[10] so the minority got some representation. The two main political parties quickly figured out how to take control and determine who is anointed in each district. Today there are still two states, Maine and Nebraska, that don't use the "winner-take-all" method.[11] Also, the presidential primaries in most states award delegates proportionately.

This winner-take-all system has served to reinforce the power of the top two political parties, since no one else can get a seat with this system (unlike European systems, where minor parties get some seats with a proportional system, forcing the forming of coalitions and– OMG– compromise). Most of us don't care about the minor parties, but it also affects Republicans and Democrats. A state with 40% Democrat voters ends up with *all* representatives being Republican, rather than just 40% of the representatives being Democrats. This sure looks like taxation without representation. The below chart[12] shows a few examples, with the results due to the combination of winner-take-all and rigging district boundaries (gerrymandering), discussed later (and affected by independents and people who don't bother to vote).

State	Republican Reps	Democrat Reps	% of registered voters that identify as Republican	% of registered voters that identify as Democrat
Alabama	6	0	44%	44%
Arkansas	4	0	36%	49%
Connecticut	0	5	30%	57%
Mass.	0	9	26%	60%
Oklahoma	5	0	42%	47%

Political parties.

There is no mention of political parties in the Constitution. There were no political parties at the time, under the Articles of Confederation. The Founders apparently hoped (alas, in vain) that national politics could be conducted without political parties. It didn't take long for political parties to dominate, after George Washington's second term. George warned against political parties in his farewell address:

> *"The alternate domination of one faction over another, sharpened by the spirit of revenge, natural to party dissension, which in different ages and countries has perpetrated the most horrid enormities, is itself a frightful despotism."* George Washington Farewell Address, 1796.[13]

There is a natural tendency to organize into groups, like street gangs. Worse, we've become loyal to our parties like our sports teams. What is reprehensible if done by the other gang is just and proper if done by your gang. We need to recognize that and agree a foul is a foul, no matter who commits it.

> *"There is nothing which I dread so much as a division of the republic into two great parties."* John Adams, 1780.

Originally, the federal government was weak and most things were done by state and city governments. Political parties were run by corrupt bosses, such as Boss Tweed of Tammany Hall (an affiliate of the "Democratic-Republican" party in New York City & state). The bosses would recruit poor immigrants and bestow favors to control their voting. Control was achieved through patronage (government jobs), government contracts (which cause projects to cost the government much more than they should), selective enforcement of laws (e.g., Sunday liquor sales) and selective collection of taxes, all in exchange for payoffs and political support. Patronage was most famously applied to the federal government by Andrew Jackson. This same type of patronage system was rampant in Greece and Italy and led to their recent financial collapse. The civil service system we have today was put in place to end the corrupt patronage system (and gave us different problems).[14]

Political parties (national gangs) run our government. There are two main gangs, the reds (Republicans) and blues (Democrats), and they vote in blocks. Any senator or representative who shows backbone, and votes his or her conscience for the good of the country, instead of the gang agenda, is punished (the job of an "enforcer" in a street gang).

The punishment can be the lack of a committee assignment, the lack of funds for reelection, special interest negative ads or even the party supporting a primary challenger. This control of party members starts with how each party's candidates for representatives are selected. Candidates for representatives today are selected by a procedure that was originally designed as a reform against party bosses, but has led to more partisan candidates– primary elections.

Primary elections.

The primary elections enable the special interests to entrench their uncompromising true believer lackeys. Since political parties aren't mentioned in the U.S. Constitution, primary elections, which are used to select a candidate for a party, certainly aren't. National Conventions weren't even used until 1832. The delegates to the national convention were selected by state conventions, and those delegates were selected by local conventions. Those conventions were controlled by corrupt political bosses. Progressive era reforms sought to remove the influence of the bosses, and established primary elections to do this. The first primary didn't occur until 1910. Some states established primaries after 1910, but then went back to the parties choosing delegates. Up until 1968, only 20 states had primary elections. The impetus for most states to adopt primaries was the 1968 Democratic National Convention, where Vice President Hubert Humphrey was nominated with the support of the party bosses, even though primary victories and other shows of support indicated that Senator Eugene McCarthy (with an anti-Vietnam War campaign) had more popular support.

Today, some states have primaries (run by local government), others have caucuses (run by the parties), at different times between January and June of a general election year. Iowa and New Hampshire, the #30 and #42 states in term of population,[15] have an outsized effect due to being the first caucus/primary. Iowa uses its position to extort promises to maintain the ethanol (made from corn) subsidies enriching the state's corn farmers, with questionable environmental benefits.[16]

The long time between the first primary and the general election has led to endless campaigning, requiring more money from special interest contributions (and thus more influence). Fundraising begins anew the first day in office, especially in the House, where terms are only 2 years. The Founders didn't see this coming.

Nearly half of Americans don't vote in general elections (perhaps they realize, due to winner take all rules, that their vote doesn't count). Even fewer people (the most fervent) vote in primaries, which results in the most ideological, non-compromising candidates being elected. To win the primary, the radicals of each party need to be courted. The most radicalized voters are the ones who spend the time to get involved in their party and thus control who gets nominated (You may know some of these– the nutty neighbor who wants to shut down the government and has a bomb shelter and a tank in the backyard, or the one trying to start a commune and quotes Mao all the time). The moderates (who are willing to compromise to get things done) are outvoted simply because they don't show up for the primary.

The moderates are also outvoted in the general election because by then the moderate candidates have already been weeded out. Since more people pay attention to presidential candidates than Congressional candidates, the nut-cases do get weeded out of the presidential election – well, most of the time. The candidate for the dominant party in that district will get elected, regardless of his/her positions on the issues. The results of the radicalization brought on by our primary system are evident in our polarized Congress. This effect of primary elections is compounded by how representatives are elected and district boundaries are drawn.

How representatives are elected.
The US Constitution doesn't specify how representatives are elected. It simply says each state gets at least one, apportioned according to the number of people in the state, and requires a

census every 10 years to reallocate the number of representatives for each state due to changes in population. It doesn't even mention districts or district boundaries. As noted above, in the early years of the United States most states originally elected representatives at large, without districts– essentially one large multi-member district. The Constitution gives the state legislatures the power to set the rules for elections (e.g., single or multi district). Congress actually has the power to overrule them[17] – but never has. The political parties, once in control of a state legislature, set district boundaries to rig elections to increase their stranglehold at both the state and federal level.

Setting district boundaries.

The Constitution doesn't say how district boundaries are to be set; it simply says that each state legislature can set its own rules. Almost all state legislatures give this power to– surprise– themselves. Whichever party has control of the legislature after the census sets the boundaries to benefit their party. You may have heard of "gerrymandering." The word "Gerrymander" comes from Massachusetts governor Elbridge Gerry signing a bill in 1812 that redrew the districts in the Boston area in the shape of a salamander. This gave an advantage to his Democratic-Republican Party (the parties were different back then).

Above, original Gerrymander map from 1812 Boston Gazette.

Gerrymandering is used by the party in power to increase the number of representatives from their party. Russia, Venezuela and other countries jail the opposition– we're just a bit more sophisticated. Gerrymandering is done by cramming all the other party voters in a few districts, wasting their votes where they already have a majority. This takes away the other party's majority in all the other districts by relocating the number of voters over 50% in most districts into a few voter refugee camp districts. Thus, a state where the majority of voters are Republican can end up with the majority of the representatives being Democrats. Not only does this tactic increase the number of seats for the party in the majority, it results in more radical candidates. Because each district now has a clear majority, instead of being evenly split, candidates only need to appeal to the voters of the majority party in that district (amplifying the radicalizing effect of primaries to elect uncompromising zealots). The effect is worse for the districts where the opposition has been jammed, with super-majorities.

Recent trends have made this worse with sophisticated mapping software developed in the 1990s. Such software has even been used to move the district lines so that the home of an incumbent of the other party is no longer in the district, making that incumbent ineligible to run for reelection in that district (rumor has it that a Trump software upgrade will enable moving the location on birth certificates of presidential candidates out of the country).

As a result of the toxic brew of party primaries, winner-take-all districts and Gerrymandering, well over 90% of seats are solidly Democratic or Republican, safe for the incumbent[18]. Today the incumbent's party wins almost all the time, hitting a high of 99% in 2004.[19]

There has been a lot of press on the structure of our Electoral College and winner-take-all system making it possible to win the popular vote, yet not become president. Presidents who were elected, even though they lost the popular vote, were John Quincy Adams (1825), Rutherford B. Hayes (1877), Benjamin Harrison (1889), and most recently in 2000, George Bush (over Al Gore).[20] Less known, and perhaps more significant, is that the same thing happens in Congress. The Senate, of course, is by design not representative of the majority. After the 2010 census, the Republican majorities in many state legislatures took Gerrymandering to a new level with the Republicans REDMAP initiative (REDistricting MAjority Project).[21] The 2012 elections produced a sizeable Republican majority (234-201) in the House, even though a majority of the country voted for Democrats.[22] That Republican majority increased to 247 in the 2014 elections (with lower voter turnout).[23] The Democrats have done the same when they've been in control.[24] Our system makes many people feel disenfranchised. They don't bother to vote because they feel their vote doesn't count. They are right. Our system has thus been warped from voters picking the representatives they want to representatives picking the voters they want.

Election rules.

Gerrymandering is enhanced if the number of people who vote is also controlled. If the number of the other party who vote is reduced, fewer people need to be packed in refugee camp districts. In 1845, Congress established the first Tuesday after the first Monday in November for federal elections. At that time, the U.S. was mostly farmers without today's work week and free weekends, and a weekday avoided voting on the Jewish Sabbath (Saturday) or Sunday.[25] Many people have difficulty leaving their jobs to vote during the week, and thus the use of Tuesday limits voter turnout. After the Civil War, southern states imposed a variety of rules to suppress the Black vote– literacy tests, poll taxes, property-ownership requirements, moral character tests, etc. The Voting Rights Act of 1965 attempted to stop this, and one provision was that states with a history of discrimination needed federal approval for new voting laws. The Supreme Court struck this down in 2013, saying the country had changed dramatically and that this was no longer necessary. Immediately after the decision, a number of southern and other states enacted new voting laws that would restrict turnout by Blacks and the poor, such as restricting when registration was possible, requiring more documents to register, and limiting or ending early voting. If this wasn't motivated by racism, it was certainly motivated to provide advantages to the Republican Party, since Blacks and the poor tend to vote for Democrats.[26]

For their part, Democrats have defeated many measures to have local elections at the same time as federal elections. Apparently, this lowering of voter turnout favors Democrats, since the motivated voters are the government workers and union members affected by the local issues.[27] Many other countries not only make it easier to vote, but have compulsory voting, such as Australia.[28]

This gerrymandering and voter suppression, combined with the fact that only the most dedicated (and thus radical) of each party vote in the primaries, has caused the virtual extinction of yet another species on Earth– the moderate representative. This gaming of the system not only elects radicals, thus polarizing the parties; it further increases the chances the President and

Congress will be controlled by different parties. But the real power is behind the scenes. This system entrenches not just incumbents from the different parties, but the special interests that provide their funding.

Campaign fundraising.

Campaign fundraising is not addressed in the Constitution, and has become probably the biggest corrupting influence in our political system. Reform is supported by both progressive Democrats and the conservative Tea Party.[29] The progressive Democrats and the working class of the Republican Tea Party both criticize the corrupting influence of dependence on support from Wall Street and banks. The rich should also be concerned, because the effects lead to a weakening of the economy.

The need for campaign fundraising provides a carrot and stick to special interests. Lobbying influence is greatly enhanced by the need for representatives to raise large amounts of cash to run a campaign. Representatives can't close the door on the lobbyist/donors who are funding their campaign (would you close the door on the person paying all your expenses?). They lobby for unfair special breaks that the rest of us pay for. Democrats and Republicans can agree on stopping many of these, but they are shackled by their special interest overlords. For example, off-shore tax havens cost us $184 billion/year, and various corporate subsidies cost $100 billion/year (see Appendix III). This is not just an objection of Democrats– the conservative donor Charles Koch opposes such corporate welfare,[30] and would prefer a level playing field with lower overall rates. Examples of subsidies include the ethanol fuel credit, oil and gas drilling deductions, solar subsidies and crop insurance subsidies. All these giveaways have resulted in higher tax rates on the rest of us.

Some have argued that if money is given to a candidate that already agrees with the viewpoint of the donor, then that donation is not true bribery or corruption. That may be technically correct, but only those with the same viewpoint as the special interest get funding. The result is the same– those with money are able to buy the election of politicians that support their views. Those who put the common good ahead of giving every advantage to their special interest backers don't get money and are left out in the cold.

In business, an executive gets both a salary and an expense account from the company. The executive thus knows who to please– the CEO or stockholders. In Congress, it is split. The salary of representatives ($174,000) is paid for by the government (taxpayers), while their expense accounts (campaign expenses) are paid for by special interests (average $1.3 million). They do have staff paid for by the government, but they are not allowed to work on re-election campaigns. Who do you think they will owe more fealty to? Their real bosses, who provide the vast majority of the money they need to do their jobs, are the donor/lobbyists. This has made Democrats beholden to unions and environmental groups, and Republicans beholden to the rich, the NRA and corporate groups (although once elected, special interests will give to whomever can pass the bill they want). The individual donors have been referred to as the "donor class," with 0.26% providing 67% of all federal campaign dollars (that's less than 1% of the donors, for the math-challenged).[31]

When the Constitution was adopted, TV and radio hadn't been invented, and there was no need for these huge advertising expenses. The concept of fundraising of the magnitude we have today was unknown to the Founders. In the last 40 years, the cost has skyrocketed. In 1974, the mean amount spent to run for a seat in the House was $53,000, and for a seat in the Senate it was $440,000. By 2012 it had increased to $1.2 million for House seats, and $9.3 million for Senate seats.[32] Since a Senator's government salary is $174,000, that means that 98% of the money they receive is paid by donor/lobbyists. Of note, House incumbents spent more than double what challengers spent, reflecting their greater fundraising ability. The greater fundraising ability is due to special interests wanting to gain influence with the sitting representative.[33]

It is not only the money that is a problem; it is the time and attention that representatives spend on special interests instead of the public business. Representatives spend half their time in office raising money.[34] The amount of time has doubled since the Supreme Court struck down limits on campaign fundraising in the *Citizens United* case in 2010.[35] Representatives actually trudge a few blocks from the capital to telemarketer-like cubicles in call centers to dial for dollars.[36] The other half of their time is apparently spent working on legislation that the special interest donors want. Because of the enormous amounts of money required to campaign, the short 2 year term for representatives and the early primaries, new representatives must start fundraising all over again the first day in office. We have a system that elects good fundraisers, not good legislators.

While there is a lot of focus on the huge sums spent on presidential campaigns, that is not the real problem. Obama showed the ability to fund a campaign with small donations using the Internet, raising massive amounts of money. Thus, Obama in theory should not owe fealty to special interests, except that he needs the support of his party in Congress. Also, the president, and a major presidential candidate, can draw media attention and use the bully pulpit. The same cannot be said of senators and representatives. A representative, or candidate, cannot command the same media attention, and thus needs to buy ads. When was the last time you watched a press conference with the representative of your district? Do you even know who your representative is? Only 35% of voters know the name of their representative,[37] much less his/her positions on the issues. It is the Congressional campaigns where the problem lays, and raising large sums through the Internet with name recognition, as Obama did, simply isn't possible. This need for huge campaign funds is an Achilles heel of our political system that special interests exploit.

Campaign funding is also a way to threaten representatives to keep them in line. The NRA leadership is famous for mounting negative ad campaigns to defeat any representative that dares to vote for any regulation of guns (the NRA used to be reasonable, but the leadership was taken over by a hard-liner coup in 1977).[38] The NRA leadership in 1994, for example, successfully targeted for defeat NRA card-carrying conservative Democrats who dared to vote for a 10 year ban on assault weapons (that is why it wasn't renewed in 2004). In another example, in 2012 the NRA ran attack ads against Republican Debra Maggart, who chaired the Republican caucus of the Tennessee House of Representatives. Her sin was having the temerity to kill an NRA-backed bill that would have permitted Tennesseans to keep firearms in their parked vehicles wherever they went (which

23

leads to stolen guns).[39] This negative ad threat is why, after the 2012 Sandy Hook massacre of twenty 6 and 7 year old children by a man with a history of mental illness, a bill to require background checks for criminal and mental health history for gun sales died in Congress. The bill failed in spite of support for background checks by 89% of Americans and even 75% of NRA members.[40]

The constant attacks by the NRA have also benefited the gun manufacturer members by suggesting (wrongly) that President Obama wants to take guns away from law-abiding citizens. The result? Gun sales have doubled during the Obama administration.[41]

The AFL-CIO union has done the same. For example, in 2015, they went after a Democrat, Ami Bera, who dared to support fast-track trade authority for the president against the union's wishes.[42] The union launched a series of negative ads and a guerrilla smear campaign. The message was clear to other Democrats deciding how to vote– toe the union line, or be attacked.

The wealthy members of the Club for Growth attacked moderate Republicans who didn't vote for enough tax cuts. For example, in 2012 they successfully spent $2.2 million to unseat moderate Indiana Republican Senator Dick Lugar and $700,000 to unseat moderate Nebraska Republican Attorney General Jim Bruning.[43]

In another example, Mayor Adrian Fenty of Washington D.C. appointed Michele Rhee to fix D.C.'s poor-performing schools. In 2010, the teachers union was angered when Rhee closed schools, fired principals and tried to give teachers the choice of salaries of up to $140,000 based on student achievement, but only if tenure was given up. The teachers union spent over $1 million against Fenty in his reelection campaign, defeating him and causing Rhee to leave.[44] The campaign against Fenty was a warning to other cities considering putting student interests ahead of teachers' interests.

These politicians don't have the funds or the presidential bully pulpit to defend themselves. There is no "defend your vote doing the right thing" special interest that gives money to representatives.

The special interests thus use a carrot & stick approach– the carrot is campaign contributions, the stick is negative ads if the special interest bidding isn't done. Under our system, representatives who vote for the good of the country instead of the agenda of their bosses (special interests) get fired. Since a minority or even a single senator can block action or hold a bill hostage for concessions, no action that would offend *any* special interest (whether they support Democrats or Republicans, or play both sides) can be taken without the threat of retaliation, leading to the inability of Congress to do anything significant without it being riddled with exceptions or concessions for the special interests.

The system of government we have in the US encourages corruption. It is similar to the early days of baseball, when players could be bribed to throw a game by gamblers because the payoff was much higher than their salary. Higher baseball salaries today make them much less susceptible to bribery, but salaries of representatives and senators are low compared to equivalent positions in business. The salaries are miniscule compared to campaign expenses. This system for Congress is like telling police officers they need to buy their own police cars, guns and uniforms, and letting them raise the money by shaking down businesses for protection money. Once the special interests have the undivided attention of representatives through contributions, the door for lobbying is wide open.

Lobbying.
Lobbying is actually mentioned in the Constitution, in the First Amendment's guarantee of the right of free speech and the right to petition the government. Although lobbying has always been a fact of life, professional lobbying has exploded recently, with the total amount spent on lobbyists going from $100 million in 1975[45] to $3.21 billion in 2015.[46] Note this only includes direct lobbying, and not the huge sums spent influencing voters, to get them to lobby their representatives in the interests of the lobbyists' clients. For example, special interests use "astroturf

lobbying" to create apparent grassroots campaigning and apparent public support for a cause (form letters to send to Congress, supposedly independent email campaigns, etc.).[47]

Common sense tells us that they wouldn't be spending these sums unless it works. Today, lobbyists openly tout on their websites the huge return on investment from tax lobbying. Representatives also become cozy with lobbyists since many depend on employment with lobbyists after leaving office, where they earn much bigger salaries (an average 1452% pay raise[48]). In 1974, 3% of retiring members of Congress became lobbyists. By 2013, that had increased to 50% of retiring Senators and 42% of retiring House members.[49]

While the media places more emphasis on campaign financing, that is actually just the ante to sit at the lobbying table. Special interests spend much more money on lobbying than on campaign contributions.[50]

JUDICIARY   **CONGRESS**

Congressional staff.

Congress is increasingly reliant on lobbyists for expertise in different areas, since Congress doesn't have enough experienced staff. Senators and Representatives don't get enough expertise from their staff and committee meetings, and instead are briefed on issues by lobbyists – the very people they raise money from.[51] In an effort to show voters they are trying to contain costs, Congress has cut its own staff by 20% between 1979 and 2015, despite increasing complexity and workloads.[52] Because Congressional staff salaries are much lower than industry salaries, the staff is young and inexperienced– most staffers with experience move on to better-paying jobs.[53] While the staff reductions have saved some money and provided political talking points, the cuts have cost much more money due to giveaways to special interests.[54]

This influence gained by special interests from their contributions and lobbying can be exercised by taking advantage of some odd voting procedures adopted by Congress.

Voting procedures for Congress.

The Constitution does not set forth voting procedures for Congress.[55] The Founders left it to Congress to adopt its own rules on voting procedures over the years. The Senate stands out for adopting a series of bizarre rules. The result is that each senator today has much more power than intended under the Constitution. There are only two senators per state, and each apparently has an exaggerated sense of self-importance and thinks he/she should be president and have veto power over every bill.

Senate Filibuster.

The filibuster (endless talking by a senator to stop a vote) is not in the Constitution and did not exist when the US was founded. It was first used in 1837.[56] It has been defended as a rarely-used tool to allow the minority to block things they felt strongly about (e.g., keeping slavery, blocking civil rights). The Senate eventually added a rule to end a filibuster (cloture), but it requires a 60% vote. Thus, a single Senator can increase the requirement for passage of any bill from 50% to 60%.[57] This was not intended by the Founders.

Before 1970, there were less than 10 filibuster cloture votes a year; by 2008 it passed the 100/year mark[58]. Today filibusters are used to simply block action by the majority party, or action that some special interest supporter of a senator doesn't like. There has been some small progress. In 2013, the Democratic controlled Senate changed the filibuster rules to eliminate the filibuster for executive branch and judicial nominees, except for the Supreme Court. This was in response to the Republicans holding up large numbers of nominees of President Obama (of course, when the Democrats were in the minority during George Bush's administration, they did the same thing). The filibuster upsets the careful balance designed by the Founders, and allows special interests to block action with influence over a single senator.

Senate holds on bills.

The Senate rules allow a single President-wannabe senator to prevent a bill from reaching a vote on the Senate floor. This is not in the Constitution. They are also not a part of the formal "standing rules," and are simply a "courtesy" (supposedly a courtesy to other senators, but really a courtesy to special interests while an affront to the public). They are extremely effective in allowing a single senator to stall legislation. The original intent of the rule was to ensure a senator would be consulted on legislation that affected the senator's state or was of particular interest to a senator. The hold provided time to study the proposed legislation, and postpone a vote. Holds didn't become common until the 1970s as the Senate changed from a collegial body to today's more partisan Senate where senators will exploit the rules for their benefit.

Holds are used to get concessions for special interests or states. They are usually secret, although a few have come to light. For example, in 2003, Senator Larry Craig of Idaho put a hold on 850 Air Force promotions, holding them hostage to get cargo planes for the Idaho Air National Guard.[59] Holds are used not just against bills a senator doesn't like, but as retaliation or extortion to get the sponsor of the held bill to vote for the holder's bill. It is as if two year olds designed the Senate rules.

Since the rules were changed to end anonymous holds[60] and require the entering of the senator's name into the public record after two days, a common approach to maintain anonymity was a 'tag-team' approach. A first senator (anonymously) places a hold, but releases it before the 2 day publication requirement. A second senator then does the same. The first senator repeats the hold for two days, and so on indefinitely. In 2011, the Senate amended the rules to eliminate secret holds and the "tag-team" approach, but holds are still used to block legislation, and the anti-secrecy rule is apparently not enforced[61]. With a hold possible by a single senator, a lobbyist has yet another way to stop a bill using a connection to a single senator. But stopping bills is only half the game. Sometimes special interests want to pass a bill that benefits them.

Unrelated amendments ("Christmas Tree Bills").

Senators are not limited by the germaneness (same subject) rule present in the House and are able to add unrelated "riders" (amendments) to bills. This is not in the Constitution. This is often done to provide benefits to special interest campaign contributors. Since this became common in the rush of bills before Congress adjourns for the Christmas holidays, they have been called Christmas tree bills– everyone got a present (every special interest, that is– the rest of us get a lump of coal and the presents put on our tab). Originally, the bills were attached to tax bills to provide specific tax or trade benefits to an industry. Sometimes they were more targeted, such as the 1986 Tax Reform Act which granted a tax exemption to any "corporation incorporated on June 13, 1917, which has its principal place of business in Bartlesville, Oklahoma" (Phillips Petroleum).

The practice expanded in the 1980s. Instead of amending just tax bills, riders were added to huge omnibus bills to hide them from public scrutiny. Continuing resolutions to keep the government operating without a budget became a favored target. This is a gold mine for special interests.

By attaching the riders to popular or important bills, it makes it difficult for the President to veto them. The President does not have a line-item veto, unlike many state governors (Congress passed a law to give the president a line-item veto in 1996 to control pork barrel spending, but it was held unconstitutional by the Supreme Court in 1998 in *Clinton v. City of New York*). Another tactic is to attach a rider to a popular bill to force an opponent to vote against it, and then use that vote in an attack ad. For example, Republicans attached a defunding of Planned Parenthood to a government budget funding bill[62] and Democrats tried to attach riders to the Keystone pipeline bill to require clean energy jobs and the use of US manufactured steel.[63] Then they can then truthfully say the Democrats voted to cause a government shutdown and Republicans voted against the Keystone Pipeline.

These Senate rules not only give each senator more power, they also give special interests more power because there are more "choke points" that can influence or stop legislation. Lobbyists don't need to influence a majority of the senators, and they certainly don't need to influence a majority of the voters. Just a few senators, or even one, will do. The senators (and their special interests) love having this power, and won't give it up easily. Since all the favors to special interests cost money– a *lot* of money– who do you think pays for it?

Changes that crippled compromise.

Congress has a history of addressing minor matters to score political points, while ignoring larger matters. For example, spending cuts are usually made to the discretionary budget, while ignoring safety net programs (Social Security, Medicare, etc.), defense and the deficit interest payments which together make up 83% of the budget (see appendix III).

Earmarks.

An earmark is a provision that directs approved funds to be spent on specific projects. They have been criticized as pork-barrel spending. Earmarks were banned by a House rule in 2011, after controversy over the 2005 "bridge to nowhere" earmark ($223 million for a bridge to a small Alaskan town attached to a Hurricane Katrina reconstruction bill).[64] However, an unintended consequence was making it more difficult to compromise and get votes to pass bills. Although unsavory, there is a long history of such horse trading of relatively minor expenses to accomplish larger goals. If you watched Daniel Day Lewis in the 2012 Steven Spielberg movie "Lincoln," you know the approval of the 13th amendment banning slavery required horse trading of federal jobs to lame-duck congressmen.[65] LBJ got support from the House Republican leader for the 1964 Civil Rights Act by giving a NASA research grant to the leader's district.[66] While directing a project to a specific contractor is a recipe for corruption, directing already approved funds to particular projects in a state or district is much less so, and may be a necessary smaller evil to achieve a larger good. Also, earmarks constitute less than 1% of the U.S. budget.[67]

Transparency.
In the wake of the Watergate scandal in 1973, Congressional committee meetings have been public, and C-SPAN cameras record practically everything. This has had the unintended consequence of making it difficult to compromise and grandstanding for the voters. Compromise requires making concessions that true believer constituents watching on TV will not like. While transparency to see what special interests are influencing Congress is good, transparency that prevents reaching across the aisle to make a deal is not.[68]

"The idea that Washington would work better if there were TV cameras monitoring every conversation gets it exactly wrong." Tom Daschle, former Democratic Senate majority leader (2014).

Committees.
Committees are where members of opposite parties get to know each other and are forced to work with each other, good conditions for compromise. Since the 1970s, there have been reforms in Congressional procedures to shift power away from committees and to the rank-and-file, to provide a more democratic process. However, an unintended consequence is that power has shifted to the party leaders, who have become more partisan and less willing to compromise.[69] Another feature of committees is that members tend to get appointed to committees

34

they are interested in. This results in farm state representatives on the agriculture committee and defense hawks on the armed services committee,[70] with the foreseeable result of proposals to spend more money in those areas.

Budget Deficit.

The U.S. Constitution doesn't require a balanced budget.[71] The federal government has run a deficit since inception, when it took on debt incurred to fight the revolutionary war, including debt incurred by the states.[72] But the debt used to get paid down in between wars, and we didn't have deficit spending in peacetime (with the big exception of the Great Depression).

As of 2016, the total US debt was over $19 trillion (in 1990 it was $3 trillion). Running up the debt means passing the buck to future generations. Representatives must appeal to and appease current voters (or actually current special interests), not future ones. Politicians can cut taxes to get reelected because they have found a patsy that will foot the bill and not complain– children and the unborn. This is worse than giving a teenager a credit card.

Thus, we often see benefits provided to current special interests, while the burden of paying for it is put off into the future– on our children. It's like buying a sports car and agreeing that your children will pay for it. We as parents and grandparents are basically getting our current and unborn children to co-sign and be responsible for loans to pay for all the special interest giveaways and everything we are underfunding today– our Medicare payments, military, pensions, etc. Congress likes to pass popular spending bills without passing unpopular taxes needed to pay for them.

Accrual Accounting.

Deficit spending is made easy because there is no requirement for the government to show how much future expense is being taken on (accrual budgeting). A cash budget is used, showing taxes collected and payments made that year.[73] It doesn't show, as accrual accounting would, most future payment obligations incurred by new laws today. It also doesn't show increased payments in the future due to demographic changes. For example, Social Security works today because there are enough current workers to pay for the smaller number of retirees. However, when the bulk of the baby boomers retire, there won't be enough workers, and when the young today retire, there won't be enough money left.[74] If the government were forced to use accrual accounting, the politicians would have to explain how they will be able to pay for the obligations taken on.

The Social Security fund *"is expected to decline steadily until the trust funds are depleted in 2034"* and the Medicare Hospital Insurance Fund *"is expected to decline in a continuous fashion until reserve depletion in 2028."* Social Security and Medicare Boards of Trustees 2016 Summary Report.[75]

The $19 trillion U.S. debt doesn't even reflect many future underfunded payment obligations that would be shown with accrual accounting (e.g., $26.7 trillion in unfunded future Social Security obligations, $28.5 trillion in unfunded Medicare obligations and $8.3 trillion in federal retirement and other costs),[76] and the true debt is thus actually much, much higher – at least $82.5 trillion. Since the formation of the SEC (Securities and Exchange Commission) after the 1929 stock crash (leading to the Great Depression), the SEC has required companies to use the accrual method, not the cash method. But the government continues to use the cash method.

The lack of a true budget with accrual accounting enables special interests to get their goodies without impacting present voters, by hiding it in expenses passed on to future generations in the form of debt. This happens at the state level as well. For example, in 1999 the California Legislature incurred tens of billions of dollars in debt for retroactive pension increases to public employees without having to reflect it in the budget and face public scrutiny.[77]

"This lack of [accrual accounting] accountability creates an incentive for elected officials to curry favor with today's voters at the expense of tomorrow's taxpayers. This lack of accountability has long been a root cause of fiscal mismanagement within the U.S. government." Arthur Anderson's 1986 report "Sound Financial Reporting in the U.S. Government."[78]

II. Power Struggle Due To Lack Of Constitutional Guidelines.

THE CONSTITUTION'S DESIGNED divided government, combined with leaving implementation details to Congress and the states, has led to the political parties trying to increase the power of whatever branch of government they happen to control at the time. This provides even more opportunities for special interest influence. The careful system of checks and balances in the Constitution has been upended, with each government entity trying to grab powers reserved for another entity or branch of government.

States.
The states want to be the federal government, especially if they are controlled by a different party than the sitting President or Congress. The biggest example of this power struggle was the Civil War. This conflict is inherent in the basic structure of the United States – as a federation of states. Similar to the European Union today, each was essentially a sovereign entity at the beginning, and they have only grudging ceded power over 200 years. This has led to a host of problems.

Congress is made up of representatives from each state, and those representatives are Constitutionally sanctioned lobbyists – for their states. Each state representative and senator is motivated to bring home the bacon to their state. If they don't, they may not get reelected. This has led to earmarks – special projects for the representative's district or state (or special interest), that are usually tacked onto a budget, appropriations, or other bill as the price of that representative's vote. Congress voted to stop earmarks in 2010 and 2012.[79] That has had the unintended consequence of making compromise and passage of bills more difficult.

While an earmark targets a specific project, there are also group giveaways. For example, projects that the Pentagon doesn't even want are still approved by Congress. Each state wants to keep jobs and keep their donor/lobbyist companies happy for these projects. The budget-busting F-35 Joint Strike Fighter, for example, has contractors in 45 states working on it. This not only dramatically drives up the cost of government projects (and thus our taxes), it makes it politically impossible to kill them when it turns out to cost too much for too little an improvement over existing fighters (by 2014 it was 7 years behind schedule and $163 billion over budget).[80] Many states and local governments actually hire private lobbyists to lobby for transportation, public works, parks, and other federal government funded projects in their location.

Crafty companies pit states and local jurisdictions against each other to provide tax breaks for local business locations that generate jobs. This was practically unheard of until states started competing for GM's new Saturn plant in 1985, which started an ugly trend. The states compete with each other in a race to the bottom that guts the tax revenue of each state. The tax burden is foisted on existing companies and taxpayers already in the state, who can then lobby for their own tax breaks, or threaten to leave for another state. Commentators debate whether these are even worth it for the states that win, with many saying no.[81] But it is clear it is a losing proposition for the states as a group– billions in tax revenue are lost with no benefit for the states collectively.[82]

Courts.

As everyone knows, the U.S. Supreme Court wants to be Congress. The Supreme Court simply assumed the power (for itself and lower courts) to declare laws unconstitutional in the 1803 case of Marbury v. Madison (ironically, where the Court ruled the act of Congress allowing Marbury to bring his claim to the Supreme Court improperly extended the Court's jurisdiction beyond what was in the Constitution). Congress did not object, allowing it to become precedent.[83] The Founders thought they had prevented Congress from going beyond the Constitution by splitting it into a House and Senate which could check each other, and also providing a President with veto power. Few other countries allow their courts to declare laws unconstitutional. Since then, the courts have assumed more and more power, often due to the inability of a deadlocked Congress to take action on important, but controversial matters.[84]

Supreme Court, appellate, and district court judges get lifetime appointments. This *is* in the Constitution– to supposedly insulate them from politics (Unfortunately, there is no insulation in the appointment process). Keep in mind that in 1787, at the time the Constitution was adopted, the average lifespan, discounting infant mortality, was less than 55, compared with 81

41

today.[85] Thus a 40 year old judge appointed in 1787 would expect to serve 15 years, but would expect to serve 40 years today. Other federal judges have specified terms– e.g., bankruptcy (14 years), tax (15 years) & magistrate (8 years) judges). Even with today's long lifespans there is an incentive to appoint younger, less experienced people to lengthen the period of influence. The presidents want to govern from the grave, and we eventually end up with judges with one foot in the grave. Judges who would ordinarily retire won't do so if the President is of the other party.

The Senate, which needs to confirm the nominations, will often delay if the Senate is controlled by another party, or the minority party may filibuster. In November 2013, the Senate rules were changed to eliminate the filibuster on certain judicial appointments (but not the Supreme Court), due to continued blocking of President Obama's nominations.

The approval of Presidential appointments to the Supreme Court has turned into an ideological circus in recent decades. The most recent escalation is Senate Majority Leader Mitch McConnell's refusal to consider *any* nomination by President Obama in the last year of his term after the death of Justice Scalia, instead hoping for a Republican president in a year. Some Republican senators who want to give Obama's nominee a hearing don't dare cross their gang leader, McConnell. There is even talk of considering Obama's nominee in a lame-duck session if a Democrat wins the presidency, with the prospect of a more liberal nominee. So clearly this is completely a crass political calculation. What will be the next escalation? Will Democrats block any Republican nomination for 4 years if there is a Republican president? The Constitution set up this deadlock by saying the President's nominations are subject to the "advice and consent" of the Senate, which is often controlled by the other party.[86]

With Obama's nominee for the Supreme Court blocked, a 4-4 split on the Supreme Court means the constitutionality of laws are being determined by the lower courts.[87]

Congress.
While the Supreme Court judges want to be Congress, representatives and senators want to be president. Especially senators. You would think the bizarre voting procedures would be enough power, but no.

Legislative veto.
The basic structure of the Constitution is that Congress passes the laws, the President and administrative branch administers them, and the courts enforce and interpret them. However, our crafty Congress over the years has encroached on the administrative powers of the President. In what has been called a "legislative veto," Congress enacts a law that gives it the right to overrule an administrative decision. For example, laws have appropriated funds for the military, but required Congressional approval (actually, just the approval of the Armed Services Committee) for any new base or real estate

transaction[88]– a nice way for representatives to hand out favors to special interests. In 1983 the Supreme Court declared the legislative veto (the subsequent required approval) unconstitutional. Legislative vetoes continue to this day, however, disguised as "accommodations."[89] Presidents are basically extorted to agree, instead of vetoing, because otherwise they can't get laws passed at all.

Congressional Agencies.

In another example of a power grab, Congress has created agencies that report to Congress, instead of the President, often duplicating the functions of executive agencies. This is another consequence of the separate election of Congress and the President, resulting in them being of different parties and at cross-purposes. It seems every Committee and most members of Congress want their own agency, and they want the agency subject to Congressional oversight. The result is an incoherent system of overlapping rules and laws, with multiple bosses (Congress and the President). For example, Congress created 51 worker retraining programs & 82 projects for improving teacher quality (even though education is actually the responsibility of the states, with education being the biggest budget item of most states).[90] The control of these agencies by representatives enables the dispensing of favors to special interests. The complexity created by so many overlapping agencies allows the giveaways to special interests to be hidden, in addition to imposing mind-boggling bureaucracy and costs on businesses & individual citizens. The Founders had wisely separated the law making and administrative functions to avoid this type of corruption, only to have their plan subverted.

Independent Agencies.

Congress has made some agencies independent of both Congress and the President. Examples are the Federal Reserve Board, the Centers for Disease Control, and NASA. Because they are isolated from politicians, it is no surprise that independent agencies have high public approval, while Congress and other agencies have low public approval ratings,.[91] The temporary, independent Base Realignment and Closure (BRAC) Commissions avoided every state fighting to keep its military bases by requiring a single vote on the entire package of closures.[92] These independent agencies have proven to be an effective way to isolate certain government functions from special interest control and pork barrel spending.

President.

While Congress wants to be President, the President wants to be Congress, and is not satisfied with the Constitutional role of administering laws passed by Congress. Voters actually want that. People today expect the President to set an agenda for the country, and naturally gravitate toward a single leader, but that wasn't the original plan. The Constitution gave Congress the power to make laws and thus set the agenda, with the President merely administering laws passed by Congress. President Teddy

Roosevelt popularized the term "bully pulpit," emphasizing the ability of the President to sway public opinion, as a way to set an agenda that Congress needs to respond to. But more recently, Presidents haven't been satisfied with just a bully pulpit. [93]

Executive Orders.

One way the President gets around Congress is with Executive Orders. By themselves, executive orders are simply the most formal way a President gives orders to his staff, the administration. The President also uses proclamations, memorandums, opinions, oral instructions, etc. Most of these orders derive directly from the President's authority under the Constitution to administer the laws.[94]

Executive orders originally were done with the support of Congress. They were used by many presidents, including George Washington (neutrality to fighting between England and France[95]), Lincoln (Emancipation Proclamation[96]), Theodore Roosevelt (new national forests[97]) and Franklin Roosevelt (New Deal executive orders[98]).

A couple early examples of the conflict to come were a Truman order to seize the Youngstown steel mills in 1952 (to stop a steel strike during the Korean war, quickly invalidated by the Supreme Court[99]), and desegregating the military (after Congress refused his proposal to do so[100]). Reagan issued executive orders to reign in government regulation, especially order 12291 in 1981 which required a cost benefit analysis of new laws & regulations (To their credit, every President since, including Clinton and Obama, have continued this requirement.[101]). Congress didn't like this, because they were accustomed to passing popular laws without having to pass unpopular taxes to pay for them. More recently, Presidents have expanded the use of Executive Orders when they are unable to get laws passed in a hostile Congress. Usually, these orders are argued to have authority under some existing law. Thus, they naturally set themselves up for review by the courts.

One example was an executive order by President Bush for military commissions to try enemy combatants at Guantanamo

Bay. It was struck down by the Supreme Court 5 years after the order was issued.[102] Such successful court challenges are rare because of the standing requirement– someone needs to show they are adversely affected to sue. Since such suits take years to reach the Supreme Court, oftentimes the order has already served the President's objective (e.g., the Civil War was over in 5 years).

Any executive order can be fairly easily revoked by a subsequent President. A later Congress can also reverse laws of an earlier Congress, but it is much more difficult. Clinton revoked or modified many of Reagan and Bush's executive orders. Reagan blocked U.S. aid to organizations providing abortion counseling. Bill Clinton reversed it, then George W. Bush reinstated it, then Obama rejected it again. Another example was Jimmy Carter limiting what government information could be classified, only to be reversed by Reagan, who was reversed by Clinton, who was reversed by Bush, who was reversed by Obama.[103]

The recent increased use of filibusters means that even with control of both the House and Senate, a President can't get laws passed and must resort to Executive Orders to get anything done. Obamacare only passed because there was briefly a filibuster-proof 60 senator Democratic majority in the Senate.

Even with a Congress of the same party, there are disagreements. Congress can overrule the President by passing a law, but that isn't as easy as it sounds. The junior Bush unsuccessfully tried to get a Republican-controlled Congress, his own party, to limit federal funding for stem cell research (where stem cells were obtained from aborted fetuses). He then issued executive order 13435 to enact the ban. That Republican Congress passed a bill reversing Bush's order in 2006, but then Bush vetoed the bill. Congress then needed a 2/3 majority, which they didn't have, to override.[104]

President Obama campaigned on the idea of bi-partisan cooperation. But faced with a Congress with an avowed goal of blocking his agenda, he eventually adopted a policy of enacting whatever he could justify with executive orders and memorandum. Examples include not enforcing the Defense of Marriage act (which denied marriage benefits to homosexual

47

couples) and implementing the "Dream Act" he couldn't get Congress to pass (to shield illegal immigrant children from deportation).[105] The new majority Republican Congress tried to reverse a follow-on order, tied to a Homeland Security funding bill. However, it couldn't get past a threatened Democratic filibuster in the Senate.[106]

Less formal than executive orders is ordinary control of the administration. For example, when President Bush couldn't get Congress to completely eliminate the estate tax, he drastically reduced the size of the IRS audit team for estate taxes, allowing the estate tax to be evaded with little chance of consequences.[107]

This is a poor way to run a government, with policies changing with every administration. Laws at least have some staying power and consistency that allow long-term planning.

Signing Statements.

Signing statements are written statements issued by the President in conjunction with signing a bill passed by Congress. Until the 1980s, signing statements were rarely used and were generally ceremonial, with a few exceptions generally directed to Congressional interference in administrative functions. For example, James Monroe (objecting to particular military appointments by Congress) and Franklin Roosevelt (Congress tried to deny compensation to 3 specific federal employees deemed subversive).[108] A common thread recently in many statements is objecting to congressional interference with administrative functions (congressional vetoes), such as requiring congressional approval for administrative tasks, congressional control over appointments, and congressional restrictions on foreign policy areas constitutionally vested in the President. Presidents Eisenhower, Kennedy, Johnson, Nixon, Ford & Carter all objected to legislative veto provisions, refusing to enforce them and/or interpreting them as requests for information. Thus, signing statements are like your spouse saying "yes, dear," but with fingers crossed.

There were a total of only 75 signing statements in nearly 200 years up to the Reagan presidency. The modern use began with Ronald Reagan, who issued 250.[109] This was part of a strategic effort, based on the opinion of legal counsel Sam Alioto (future Supreme Court justice) and Ed Meese, trying to influence the interpretation of laws (ultimately unsuccessfully– the Supreme Court wasn't buying it). Reagan, George H. W. Bush and Clinton each objected to more provisions of laws with signing statements than all the presidents before them. The recent use of signing statements reflects increased partisanship and ideological warfare. For example, a Clinton signing statement refused to enforce portions of the Telecommunications Act of 1996 that prohibited certain abortion related speech over the Internet. The younger George Bush used signing statements to object to more provisions than any president before him (1200 provisions in 223 signing statements).[110] Some controversial examples of laws he objected to, and refused to enforce, were a congressional ban on torture, a request for data on the USA Patriot Act, whistle-blower protections and the banning of U.S. troops from fighting rebels in Colombia. The practical effect of signing statements is to force lawsuits in order to get new laws implemented. This requires finding someone with standing to sue (someone hurt by the law, which is often difficult to find), and can take many years to wind through the courts.

President Obama's first signing statement was on an omnibus spending bill. The other option, vetoing, would have meant no budget for the government and a potential shutdown. The bill included provisions which required administration officials to get approval from Congressional committees for spending and reallocating funds. A 2006 ABA (American Bar Association– lawyers) task force condemned signing statements, and suggested the President just veto the bill instead. The problem is that a veto isn't practical when a bill is attached to a necessary budget bill just before the government is forced to shut down.

Vetocracy with Special Interest Advantage.
The addition of all the roadblocks described above are beyond the checks and balances built into the Constitution. This has created a series of choke points for holding legislation hostage by special interests to get the favors they want (choke points include filibusters, holds, riders, vetoes, legislative vetoes, signing statements and executive orders). This has been termed a "vetocracy" by Francis Fukuyama, Erik Black[111] & others. The fact that the choke points and the legislation are complicated and obscure allows their use by special interests under the radar and prevents effective understanding and monitoring by the public. The whole reason for the original Constitutional Convention was to end the state vetocracy of the Articles of Confederation. We seem to have now come full circle, with a special interest vetocracy.

Complexity.
Another factor leading to special interest control is that the complexity of our government plays into the hands of those with money and organization. Although special interests influence

elections, their real power is in lobbying Congress, regardless of who wins. Only groups that are well organized, with lots of money, can engage in the mundane, day-to-day lobbying of the complex intricacies of shepherding bills through Congress over the course of years. Even if a bill adverse to special interests somehow passes, they can lobby for favorable regulations under the law.

In addition to the complex way laws are enacted, with multiple choke points, the laws themselves are exceedingly complex. The average length of bills that have been enacted has increased from 2 ½ pages in 1948 to 20 pages in 2013.[112] It is worse than that, because the average is skewed by short, uncontroversial laws like renaming buildings, which comprise the vast majority of the laws that can be passed in these days of a deadlocked Congress. The Affordable Care Act was 2,400 pages. The No Child Left Behind bill of 2001 was over 1,000 pages. The Dodd-Frank financial reform law passed after the 2008 financial crisis is 848 pages long.[113]

Complexity is the friend of special interests, and the enemy of the common citizen. Special interests can lobby for hidden provisions almost no one will notice. A favorite target of special interests is the tax code, resulting in mind-boggling complexity. They lobby to modify the tax code to favor themselves, in the form of what is taxed, tax rates, loopholes (that only certain people or companies can exploit) and subsidies.

There are a number of other factors leading to undue complexity in our government, laws and regulations. Two of those factors are Congressional agencies that overlap with the executive branch, and passing unneeded laws so representatives can show voters they are doing something.[114]

We unwittingly hand the tool of complexity to the special interests. Our lack of trust in government leads to complex regulations instead of discretion. If the President is of a different party, this magnifies the lack of trust, leading to reluctance to leave the administrative details to the executive branch. As pointed out in Fukuyama's book "Political Order and Political Decay," a lack of trust in institutions leads to taking away their discretion, in order to prevent corruption, with more detailed regulations. Ironically, this leads to worse government (there is no discretion to make common sense decisions and exceptions). This leads to more calls for new laws and regulations, which makes government even less effective, leading to more disgust, leading to more rules, leading to... well, you get the idea. In California, disgust with the government has led to initiatives which hamstring the government on how taxes are used, the sentences for crimes, etc. This has taken away discretion, making the government less effective, leading to more initiatives. At the federal level, we've seen similar piling on of complex laws taking away discretion and making the government even less effective.[115]

Another effect of complexity is that our legal system has become so complex that only the rich (special interests or otherwise) can afford to hire lawyers to navigate the laws and regulations.[116] Thus they get the lion's share of the benefits of our legal system.

Some complexity is built into the Constitution, in the form of trial by jury. This drives up the costs of trials. In patent cases, the juries don't understand the technology. Any prospective juror that knows about the technology is excluded from the jury by one of the attorneys, since they will prove harder to manipulate. Each side hires an expert to explain the technology, and of course each comes to an opposite conclusion. The jury then decides based on which expert seems most believable. Or has the best smile. This is nuts. For complex antitrust cases, courts have read into the Constitution an exception to the right to trial by jury. Certainly we want juries for criminal cases, but do we really need them for suits between corporations? Most European countries don't have juries, and litigation is thus much less expensive.

In addition to giving advantages to special interests, the complexity is a drag on the economy. The cost of regulation compliance is passed on to consumers, and it has been estimated that regulations cost consumers about $2 trillion a year.[117] In one example, in order to clean the air, slow climate change and lower dependence on Mideast oil, we give loan guarantees for solar companies that fail, dictate mileage standards to the auto industry, regulate smokestacks, and have a host of other regulations. Other industries are similarly regulated with complex regulations. It would be simpler to just raise the gas tax (and lower other taxes to avoid a disproportionate impact on the poor and middle class), and let the market adjust. But this wouldn't provide all the opportunities for Congress to hand out of favors to donor/lobbyists. Manipulating us voters to oppose such a tax (even if offset by a reduction in income tax) has been child's play for special interests, given the hostility to taxes and the love affair Americans have with their cars.

Where the public *is* paying attention, or a special interest needs to engage the public to enact a law or defeat a reform proposal, complexity is again the friend of special interests. There are many examples of special interests being able to rally support by voters, even when the voters are acting against their own best interests, by confusing the voters using the complexity. Many people are against health care reform that would reduce their health care costs. People are in favor of reducing an inheritance tax that would cost them more taxes because it benefits only the richest 0.2%[118] - the other 99.8% would end up paying more (because the lack of federal revenue would have to be made up in other taxes). Keep in mind that every single tax deduction, credit, exemption, etc. that does not apply to you keeps your taxes high, preventing a cut for you, and increasing your taxes.

But even where there is no complexity, on simple issues with wide public knowledge, special interests are able to manipulate us to gain support. How do they do that?

III. Manipulation.

Manipulation Techniques.
There are a wide variety of techniques used to manipulate us– here is just a taste:

Framing.
How people react to an issue depends on how it is framed. For example, "escalation" got a bad name in the Vietnam war, leading to the use of "surge" for the Iraq war – this framing implies a brief increase in troop levels. Policies that prevent students from getting good educations are framed as protecting our hard working teachers, and individual teachers become the face of the campaign, not union leaders. Pension benefits are framed as the just due of hard working public union members, rather than focusing on who pays for them (us taxpayers) or how they compare to what the rest of us get. Only one side is getting their story out– the side with money.

When raw numbers are used, or compared to percentages - beware. For example, in the 90s articles said crime was increasing because there were more murders. This was correct. However, since the population increased by more, there was actually a decrease in the rate of crime - the percentage of the population murdered went down. Or put another way, the risk of being murdered went down.

When an unusual period is used, this is likely a manipulation of the numbers to support a desired result. For example, climate data from 1983-1996 was used to assert there was actually cooling. 1983 happened to be a hot year spike, and 1996 a cool year spike, but the trend was upward. If different years were used, such as 1980-2000, a significant upward warming trend is shown.

Doublespeak.

The doublespeak and media control of Orwell's book 1984 is a horror story to most of us, but to special interests it has become a playbook for manipulating us. Here are some actual examples:

"Clear Skies Initiative"– A bill that relaxes pollution controls.[119]

"Healthy Forests Initiative"– a bill that increases clear-cutting.[120]

"The Arizona Non-Smoker Protection Act"– It would expand where smoking is permitted to bars and segregated areas of restaurants.[121]

"Californians for Affordable Prescriptions"– the pharmaceutical industry, opposing a Calif. proposition providing prescription discounts.[122]

Repeat speak.

Special Interests know that a lie is believed if continuously repeated (there are millions of forwarded emails and internet comments which do this, and even resurface after being debunked, looking for new suckers).

But the very favorite manipulation technique is dazzling in its simplicity and effectiveness - leaving out part of the story, and only presenting one side.

We citizens complain about Congress being beholden to special interests, but we are worse. Representatives are harder to fool– they have smart staffs who will point out the other side of the story. Thus, they have to be bought off (campaign contributions) or threatened (with a negative media campaign against them). The U.S. has shifted to more direct democracy over the years– pledged electors, the direct election of senators, primaries, state initiatives, etc. The shift to more direct democracy has simply changed who special interests need to influence and control. When special interests need public support, they know how to manipulate us. Businesses use the same tools that they use for product advertising. For example, they can get us to buy foods with lots of sugar and calories by using a "No Fat!" label. But we still get fat.[123] Today, ads become the subject of news stories, which become the subject of emails, with each iteration playing looser with the facts.

I'd like to plant a thought. Think about the possibility that some of your beliefs and world views, even some that are deeply held, could be the result of your being manipulated by the media. By manipulation, I don't mean brainwashing; I mean simply that you are getting only one side of the story. Think about the possibility that you could actually be wrong about something. Perhaps that is too great a leap– imagine your neighbor's views have been created by manipulation and are wrong.

Ideally, we'd all learn to be skeptical and curious; we'd be aware we're constantly being manipulated; we'd use critical reading and listening techniques; we'd know our source (is the source funded by liberals, conservatives, or a special interest?). But we don't live in an ideal world. We're busy and we're mammals– we react to fast movements, bright colors and tasty smells. Very few of us are the ideal informed, unbiased voter.

How do special interests use these manipulation techniques and weaknesses in our system to their advantage? They obtain economic advantages over the rest of us, which the rest of us pay for. Here are some examples of how we have been manipulated to give advantages to various special interests.

Manipulation and Lobbying Examples.

The health insurance lobby has successfully manipulated us for decades, and partly as a result heath care is now over 17% of our economy (up from 5% in 1960).[124] The health insurance lobby launched a multi-million dollar "Harry and Louise" ad campaign against Clinton's proposed health care reform in 1993, suggesting the government would limit choices, and "if they choose, we lose." The ads turned public opinion, which turned votes of legislators wanting to please their voters. The reform attempted to provide universal health care by requiring all employers to provide it. It would have imposed cost controls and premium caps, which the health insurers didn't want.[125] It would keep private insurance and allow profits, just not monopolistic profits. It was defeated.

When drug companies couldn't get enough seniors to pay their high prices for drugs, they wrote Medicare Part D (prescription drug benefit) in 2003 (Republican Rep. Walter Jones of North Carolina confirmed "The pharmaceutical lobbyists wrote the bill."[126]). The law prohibits the federal government from negotiating lower drug prices, generating an estimated extra profit of $242 billion over 10 years for the pharmaceutical industry, with an investment of $130 million in lobbying[127] (An 1861% return on investment– which the rest of us pay for). In contrast, the Department of Veterans Affairs, which is allowed to negotiate drug prices, has been estimated to pay 40-58% less.[128] In one example, Zaltrap, a cancer drug, was priced twice as high as Avastin, which was just as effective. Medicare had to pay the higher price ($60,000 for a treatment regimen), with the Medicare co-pay being more than $2,000 a month, which equaled the typical total monthly income for a patient in Medicare.[129] Patients are desperate to prolong their lives, and end up spending all their savings, with many going bankrupt. Another example is the cancer drug Gleevec from Novartis– the price tripled from $28,000 a year in 2001 to

58

$92,000 a year in 2012, and the government (that's our taxes) simply has to pay the new price.[130]

Obamacare has forced insurance companies to provide medical coverage to everyone, but it took a deal with the devil (insurance companies) to get it passed. Obamacare required minimum benefit levels. Did the insurance companies lobby against this by saying it will hurt their profits? No, they ran ad campaigns about people not being able to keep the insurance policy and doctor they currently have and want.[131] The fact that new insurance policies covered more, and the ones that people supposedly would want to keep covered less, was not mentioned.

Obamacare was thus forced to maintain the role of insurance companies as toll keepers between patients and doctors. To try to pass a government single payer system would have been dead on arrival with health insurance industry opposition. Clinton didn't even try that, and still failed. Every healthcare special interest had to be bought off. The American Hospital Association successfully lobbied for heavy restrictions on physician-owned hospitals, which could cut into their business.[132] The brand-name drug lobby killed rebates in the Medicare prescription drug program and maintained a prohibition against the re-importation of U.S. drugs sold abroad. They also maintained "pay-for-delay" settlements, in which drug makers pay generic manufacturers to keep low cost generics off the market when a patent expires or is about to be invalidated.[133]

Obama originally wanted cost containment in health care reform, but basically had to give that up to get the health insurers to agree to extend coverage to those with pre-existing conditions and other uninsured. The drug industry opposed the proposed "comparative effectiveness" disclosure– not just showing the new drug is better than nothing, but that it is better than existing, less expensive alternatives. The trade group Pharmaceutical Research and Manufacturers of America (PhRMA) led the charge to kill comparative effectiveness in Obamacare (PhRMA has spent a quarter of a billion dollars since 1998 on lobbying). Obama bought the drug industry's approval of expanded coverage in Obamacare by killing comparative effectiveness and steering $200 billion in profits to the drug industry by forcing more people to buy insurance. The alternative would have been lobbying and ads by the drug industry to completely kill Obamacare, just as they killed Clinton's attempt.[134]

How did the drug companies do this? Their lobbyists talked about "rationing" and "death panels" to put the entire law at risk in order to kill the "comparative effectiveness" efforts.[135] People thus thought they were opposing rationing and death panels, not opposing comparative effectiveness. Even after Obamacare was passed, there has been lobbying to prevent future efforts to require comparative effectiveness studies and disclosures. The drug industry has initiated their own selective comparative effectiveness studies (Which drugs do you think they picked? Ones that do well or ones with better, lower cost alternatives?). Then, think tanks, like the Cato institute controlled by the rich Koch brothers,[136] run policy papers saying private industry is doing these studies, and the government should stay out of it.[137] The Cato paper is of course picked up by other news media, with the appearance of being a non-partisan think tank analysis. Another example is a paper from the American Enterprise Institute (AEI), another business-funded think tank.[138] The AEI author of the paper "The FDA Should Not Mandate Comparative-Effectiveness Trials" actually lists his affiliation with his byline, "a resident fellow at AEI. Dr. Gottlieb consults with, and invests in, branded drug makers."[139] Representatives and senators (at least those in conservative, business friendly districts) face the threat of attack ads in the next election, and a loss of campaign contributions, if they don't fall in line behind the drug company position (even though cost control may be a core value they believe in).

Why would drug companies do this? What if you had invested your life savings in a wonder drug, only to find out it is no more effective than aspirin and has some horrible side effects. But then you are told that with advertising, highlighting that this magical pain relief drug has been proven effective (but without saying no more effective than aspirin), and some key donations to Congress and lobbying expenses, you can make a billion dollars. What would you do? Well, likely you would take the high road, pull the drug and go into bankruptcy. But if it was your neighbor, he'd rationalize it as just working within the rules of the system like everyone else.

The California Teachers Association outspends all other special interests on lobbying and political contributions in California, and has a political lock on the Democratic controlled legislature. They successfully lobbied to have the state constitution amended to require a minimum of 40% of California's budget be spent on education.[140] As a result of their lobbying efforts, tenure must be provided after only 2 years on the job, and once tenure is obtained, it is almost impossible to fire an ineffective teacher (the hoops a school district must go through to fire a bad teacher are framed as reasonable sounding due process, but they cost the school districts over $200,000.[141]). When layoffs occur, which happened after the 2008 financial crisis, they must be done based on seniority, and performance can't be considered.[142] This obviously discourages good young teachers and deprives students of a better education.

Do you really think the *teachers* union is looking out for student interests, or are they looking out for the teachers' interests? It wouldn't sound good to lobby for more pay and making it impossible to fire bad teachers. Rather, everything is scripted to say they are fighting to make things better for students. Many times, the teachers' interests are aligned with student interests. But when they aren't, guess whose interests prevail?

A famous 1982 study, "A Nation at Risk," detailed the problems with our schools and suggested higher teacher salaries coupled with merit pay, among other reforms. The teachers unions supported higher pay but blocked merit pay. Since then, we have fallen behind other countries in education. The lack of merit pay discourages the best college graduates from taking up teaching, with teachers now coming from the bottom third of college graduates.[143]

At the college level, for-profit diploma mills have lobbied against college quality standards for their students to receive Federal loans, preserving their profits while their students can't get jobs. Many diploma mills get over 90% of their funding from federal government grants and loans.[144] In addition to the federal

61

loans, who do you think benefits from the rule that college loans can't be discharged in bankruptcy, while businesses can discharge all their loans? Obviously, the beneficiaries are the for-profit colleges and the banks that make the loans. Studies have shown that federal loans have actually driven up the costs of colleges, since they allow colleges to charge more.[145] This is similar to the home mortgage deduction driving up the cost of a house.

In another manipulation example, realtor and builder associations fight any attempt to limit the home mortgage deduction. "We would fight it tooth and nail," David Crowe of the National Association of Home Builders told CNBC. The real estate industry has lobbied to keep the mortgage interest deduction, spending more than $80 million in lobbying Congress in 2012.[146] Do you really think they have your interests at heart, as opposed to their members? Common sense tells you that the home mortgage interest deduction enables people to buy more expensive homes, and that in itself drives up home prices.[147] Think about it. Those reality home buying shows on TV, and your own experience, should show that agents push you to go above your budget. Everyone wants the nicest home they can afford. If the home mortgage deduction wasn't there, the prices would have to come down, because people couldn't afford them.

So the real beneficiaries are realtors and banks. It is paid for by the tax payments of renters and those with less expensive homes who don't have the benefit of those deductions. If you are a renter, you are not only subsidizing those $1 million loans through your taxes, you a paying for the resultant higher property costs through higher rents. The majority of the benefit goes to those who can buy expensive homes (see Appendix III- 38% of the home mortgage deduction dollars go to those in the top 5% of income).

ExxonMobil did not do an ad campaign saying that increased gas taxes would hurt their profits and encourage alternative energy competitors. Instead, they funded think tanks to produce papers casting doubt on the science of global warming.[148] Plus, this was while Exxon was secretly planning for climate change and studying how to adapt its Arctic operations to a warming planet.[149] As this practice became discredited and caused image problems for Exxon Mobil, the traceable donations disappeared and donations to the climate change denial think tanks started coming from groups with untraceable funding.[150]

The prison guard union is the most powerful in California after the teachers union. Do you think they would be successful with a straightforward lobbying for more jobs? No, they lobby to get tough on crime, with longer sentences, and thus more prisons– which happens to mean more jobs for their union members.[151] It has been like shooting fish in a barrel, due to the public's fear of crime and media complicity with "if it bleeds, it leads" story selection. For example, they will point to the 1994 California 3 strikes law as working– saying crime has decreased since it was implemented. What they don't mention is that crime was already decreasing prior to 3 strikes in California –due to the improving economy.[152]

Defense is nearly 20% of the US budget.[153] War profiteering has led to riches in every war (e.g., JP Morgan in the Civil War), and today we have a vaster military-industrial complex than Eisenhower could have imagined.

"In the councils of government, we must guard against the acquisition of unwarranted influence, whether sought or unsought, by the military–industrial complex. The potential for the disastrous rise of misplaced power exists, and will persist." President Dwight D. Eisenhower, farewell address, Jan. 17, 1961.

For example, just before the Soviet Union collapsed in 1989, the Soviets were developing a new class of submarine, and the US countered with the development of the Seawolf class. With the collapse of the Soviet Union, the threatened development of new Soviet subs ended, and the US navy wanted to cancel manufacturing of new Seawolf subs and use the money for other ships. General Dynamics, which made the Seawolf, did not complain that its profits would be hurt. Instead, they lobbied and initiated a letter writing campaign saying that jobs would be lost, and a strategic "industrial base" of knowledge and capability to build the subs would be lost. The real irony is that "preserving jobs" is just a way to sell it to the public and give a representative some talking points– preserving profits is the real reason. After they got the Seawolf reinstated, they laid off 11,000 workers anyway over 5 years, while achieving a 38% investment return.[154]

Lobbying for defense contracts doesn't just make arms manufacturers rich– it also jeopardizes our national security. For example, the Army doesn't want any more M1 tanks. A few years ago there were 2300 deployed, with 3000 extra sitting in storage in the California desert, and they aren't useful against most modern threats. But stopping production would affect profits from a General Dynamics factory in Lima, Ohio. A lobbying and political contribution campaign targeting the 4 defense-related Congressional committees got Congress to add this back to the budget, forcing the Army to cut sought-after future weapons programs (more important to national security) to keep within the defense budget limits (possible future jobs/profits don't have the current stakeholders to lobby like current jobs). Similar lobbying got Congress to add C-17 planes the Air Force didn't want, to preserve jobs (profits) at an aircraft plant in California, and forcing cuts to the R&D program for the airborne laser the Air Force *did* want (the airborne laser program was later canceled after yearly budget changes like this by Congress, due to lack of funds, after a single successful prototype was developed and mothballed). Congress also added large ships the Navy didn't want, forcing cuts to the program for smaller boats that the Navy did want.[155]

Tax cuts.

Complex laws and regulations are the friend of special interests, allowing them to sneak in provisions unnoticed. Their favorite playground is the US tax code. The US has the highest corporate tax rate in the world on paper – the rate that applies to every business equally. However, there is a huge variance in practice because of loopholes that favor particular industries or even particular companies. Companies with the benefit of lobbying for subsidies, loopholes and other tax breaks pay little or even no tax, increasing the burden on the rest of us and the businesses which pay their fair share. Companies can make a much larger return on investment from tax lobbying than from making products– an astounding 22,000% rate of return.[156] Thus, they shift money from R&D to lobbying. Asking for a government payment would create a firestorm of protest. But it is easy to lobby for a tax loophole instead. This enables obtaining support by manipulation of the public (which hates taxes). It is framed as a tax cut to blunt opposition, but costs the same amount of your tax dollars as a direct payment. Once obtained, they are like the living dead, impossible to kill. Any attempt to take them away is framed as a tax increase. Eliminating special interest tax loopholes and subsidies is an area where the conservative Charles Koch agrees with the liberal Bernie Sanders:

> *"The senator [Bernie Sanders] is upset with a political and economic system that is often rigged to help the privileged few at the expense of everyone else, particularly the least advantaged. He believes that we have a two-tiered society that*

increasingly dooms millions of our fellow citizens to lives of poverty and hopelessness. He thinks many corporations seek and benefit from corporate welfare while ordinary citizens are denied opportunities and a level playing field.

I agree with him.[157] Charles Koch, 2016

How did the 2003 Bush tax cuts get passed when the major beneficiaries were the rich, while the rest of us or our children are inevitably going to end up paying for them because of the huge deficit being built up? Most voters focused on the tax cut they would get, and not the fact that most of the money was going to the rich and would have to be paid back by their kids.[158] Or they thought they all would be rich someday. The country had a budget surplus from the Clinton years at the time, so it seemed affordable (and a good idea at the time to keep the government from increasing spending with the available surplus). But when the Iraq war was started and the surplus disappeared, the cuts were already entrenched. At that point, special interests just needed to block a new law re-instating them, which can be done with a minority as pointed out above. Plus, they could frame it as a tax increase.

WHAT VOTERS HEAR

Many of the super-rich make most of their money from capital gains and dividends on their stock investments instead of working for a salary. They could lobby for lower taxes than the taxes on salaries earned by the rest of us by working hard. But that wouldn't go over very well. They could propose to limit the low capital gains rate to true investment in equipment, and not include stock changing hands. But that wouldn't give them the benefit they want. Instead, they get some institute they funded to publish a paper saying that capital gains tax cuts are needed to stimulate the economy, to lift all boats (but they leave out that it's not enough to offset the lost tax revenue).[159] Hedge fund managers pay themselves with capital gains ("carried interest") and thus pay lower taxes than people working for a salary.[160] It is easy to get people to support a lower capital gains tax because many of us have stocks or other investments. But what we need to recognize is that our small portion of the capital gains benefits still puts most of us on the losing end – 95% of the benefit goes to those making $200,000/year or more (See Appendix III). Guess who pays for this with high income tax rates.[161]

Another example is the inheritance tax. One of the benefits of the inheritance tax, other than to raise money, is to avoid creating a new aristocracy, correcting the unfair advantages of pure capitalism. We fought our revolutionary war to get away from such hereditary aristocracies, only to see a host of new ones created.

A lobbying campaign to repeal the inheritance tax talked about farmers losing the family farm due to inheritance tax (framed as the evil "death tax," to make people think of it negatively). What isn't mentioned is that only about 20 small businesses and farms a year owe any estate tax at all, and the estate tax allows spreading payments over 15 years at low interest rates for the rare family business or farm that has a tax and can't pay the full tax up front. The fact that the first $5 million is excluded, along with the family home for a widow, etc., isn't mentioned. Another thing not mentioned is that repeal would mean $32 billion in lost tax revenue a year the rest of us would end up paying for, and that estates worth $20 million or more would receive 73% of the benefit.[162]

These are all examples from the manipulation playbook. Some benefit to the voters is found and focused on, while the vast majority of the benefit is for some special interest. They wouldn't be spending the money on the ad campaign unless they stood to make much more money than the ad campaign would cost. We are manipulated because we naturally focus only on the effect on ourselves, plus we can only hear what is said (not what is left out). The net result is money moving from our pockets to the special interests, enriching them and impoverishing us.

A huge infrastructure has been built up to manipulate us. The media is bombarded with biased content from not only ads, but special interest think tanks. These think tanks put out studies that benefit those funding them, and are picked up by the media. The Internet has spawned multitudes of biased, sensationalist, fact-distorting blogs. Their content is copied and forwarded even after being debunked, like a world of the living dead. Email and social media campaigns are waged, giving the appearance they are grassroots campaigns started by ordinary people or experts, but are really special interest groups "astroturf" campaigns.

After decades of manipulation by special interests, there is less need to manipulate. People have internalized as core beliefs what they have been manipulated to believe. People aren't paying attention or don't have much knowledge about government beyond the sound bites they have been fed. Many people only have the attention span of a 140 character tweet. Perhaps you know someone like that. Even smart, well-read people are manipulated, more easily than you'd think.

The special interests can't manipulate everyone the same way, but enough people are polarized into separate camps to provide each special interest its core of support. That influence is magnified, since the highly polarized are the ones most likely to vote in primaries, and Gerrymandering concentrates and magnifies their influence. Once the special interest benefits are entrenched, they are difficult to dislodge. Our political system makes it easy to influence a minority that can block any legislation taking away special interest giveaways.

IV. Media

WHY DOESN'T OUR RENOWNED independent media – the 4th estate– expose these manipulations? For direct democracy to work, voters need good information to make an informed decision. Thus a robust and independent media is essential. We have neither.

The media used to be our guardians, with investigative reporting. Now, the news media is largely entertainment and an unwitting pawn of special interests. There are good programs, websites and news reports, but they are the minority and most people can't find them– they can't sort them from the chaff. The big ones we know have sold their souls.

The media is not controlled by a dictator or fake president as in some other countries, but it is still manipulated by our rulers– the special interests. In the US, due to the ability of the minority to control legislation, control of the media isn't needed– it is sufficient to manipulate a portion of the media & influence enough people to keep the majority from taking action. We are partly– or mostly– to blame. We want to read the sensational stories and be entertained, and largely don't read the balanced, probing reporting when it is done– it's too bland. In the robber baron era, citizens would attend lectures and read monthly investigative articles in magazines like McClure's. Their alternative was to watch the grass grow; they didn't have distracting smart phones and social media with its instant gratification.

The media has also undergone immense consolidation, and is now even more driven to make profits, which means providing entertainment, not news. It means pandering to the beliefs of niche viewers to keep ratings high - not challenging them. In 1983, only 50 companies controlled most of the media in the U.S. By 2012, it had been reduced to 6 companies controlling 90% of the media.[163] The consolidated media companies are pressured by shareholders to improve profits. They have thus cut the costly investigative reporting staffs that have been government watchdogs throughout U.S. history.[164] This has improved short-term profits but ironically at the expense of their brands for quality, and left them vulnerable to competition from the Internet. The large media companies have lobbied for exceptions to merger prohibitions under the antitrust laws (enforced by the Department of Justice, "DOJ," and the Federal Trade Commission, "FTC"). They argue that consolidated companies have more reporting resources and the economies of scale to compete. But they cut reporting anyway to improve short-term profits, to the detriment of our democracy.[165]The media now reports to stockholders, not to the public.

The Donald Trump campaign has capitalized on the media's quest for cheap profits. It is easier to get more eyeballs with stories about insults between candidates than substantive issue analysis. Few good people want to run for office and subject themselves to the personal attacks and media scrutiny of their personal lives. We thus get the candidates that thrive in such an environment.

Various news shows cater to people with particular viewpoints. Fox News caters to conservatives, and MSNBC caters to liberals. Each of us self-selects the news we want to watch, and thus have our views reinforced rather than challenged. Have you ever been to a party and wondered where on Earth someone was getting their news? Of course, only their news source is biased– yours is balanced. Right? We're human– we hear what agrees with our beliefs, and we tune out what doesn't.

V. It's The Economy, Stupid.[166]

SPECIAL INTEREST ADVANTAGES are on top of inherent advantages.

So there it is. The system is a mess. As a result, we pay higher taxes while special interests get the breaks. But it goes beyond this– the economy is rigged. Special interests obtain unfair *political* advantages that translate into unfair *economic* advantages. The special interest control of our government has taken advantage of the weaknesses of our system as described above to shape the economy to their advantage and our detriment. It amplifies, instead of offsetting, the inherent advantages of those with money. It concentrates wealth, crippling the consumer end of our consumer-based economy. It will eventually collapse our economy unless checked.

Our capitalistic system is inherently tilted to begin with. Don't get me wrong, capitalism is the best economic system. Communism or socialism, in contrast, has failed. The basic communist premise of providing equal pay to everyone regardless of effort or merit provides no incentive to work hard or innovate, and thus discourages extra performance– like our pay system for teachers. Such a system requires detailed government planning and extensive regulation. The government not only dictates the rules, as under Capitalism, but all the plays in the game. I think we all know how well that works.

Capitalism, however, is susceptible to unfair influence. Capitalism requires government regulation in order to function: to set the rules of the game and provide referees (enforce contracts, etc.). Those economic rules and referees (Congress) can be influenced due to the way our political system operates.[167]

We've all heard the expression it takes money to make money. That is because to start a business, the business needs to raise money from wealthy investors for a facility lease, equipment, etc. The driving mission of business is to then increase profits for the investors (who provide the capital) by increasing productivity– which means cutting costs (e.g., replacing workers with computers and making the remaining workers do more for less money). This is just the way the economy works. Our capitalistic economic system inherently favors those with capital (money). Thus, the name *capitalism* (it's not called *laborism* for a reason). It is no surprise that capital has grown faster than wages.[168] For most U.S. workers, real wages after inflation have been flat for decades, while corporate profits have boomed.[169]

Pure capitalism, like a nuclear explosion, has tremendous power but is inherently self-destructive. It has a tendency to concentrate wealth, stifling smaller competitors and impoverishing most people, leading to the destruction of the middle class, the engine of a consumer economy.[170] Intervention by lobbying the government to obtain extra advantages makes it worse. Absent government enforcement of the rules, this eventually leads to economic decline and potentially either revolution or dictatorship. This isn't in the long term best interests of anyone, including businesses and the rich. However, a properly regulated market, like a nuclear reactor, provides energy to everyone. Over regulate, and its power is diminished or extinguished.

Capitalism needs a large middle class to thrive. The wealth needs to be spread around for our consumer economy to function. If only the rich have most of the money, they only spend so much. The rest they invest– in companies which need the rest of us to have enough money to buy their products. Just as the body needs blood circulating to survive, the economy needs money circulating to survive.

Winner-take-all economy.

In addition to the inherently tilted playing field, there is another inherent characteristic that leads to unfair advantage. Our current economy has evolved to what Robert Frank & Philip Cook call the "Winner-Take-All Society" in their 1996 book with that title.[171] We are all familiar with the phenomena of the very best in sports and entertainment making much, much more money than others in those fields who are very good, but aren't superstars (or are actually as good or better, but with less luck or marketing). Frank & Cook point out that due to technology, globalization, our ability to remember only a few names, and self-reinforcing processes ("success begets success"), a select few in many fields get the most business and the most money. Everyone wants to use the best attorney when they get sued or arrested, use the best accountant, have the best CEO. We all read the bestseller books, watch the best movies and TV shows that others are talking about, etc. Through the Internet, the reach of the best is now global. The pay difference between the World Series MVP and a minor league player is enormous, as is the pay difference between a solo practitioner attorney and a partner in a big New York law firm, or, as we all have heard, between a

CEO's pay and a file clerk's pay. To the extent luck is involved in fame– and it usually plays a part – it could be called a lottery economy. It's a natural consequence of capitalism, but that doesn't make it fair - or sustainable.

It takes eternal vigilance not just to preserve freedom, but to preserve the middle class and keep a fair economy. The right government rules not only support capitalism, they save capitalism from its excesses. Americans have a storied history of fighting to keep the playing field level, and of offsetting the inherent tilt.

Monopolies and other excesses of Capitalism.
The industrial revolution led to enormous concentration of wealth in the robber barons of the late 1800s. They used the new government-granted limited liability of corporations to eliminate the personal downside of risky ventures. They secured special treatment in the form of government contracts, railroad land and mining rights. With this, they strangled the competition, forced people to buy goods at company stores and work with dangerous machinery, used child labor, hired thugs to beat union organizers, etc. Farmers were caught between bankers' usurious interest rates and the predatory, monopolistic prices of grain elevator operators and railroads.[172] But the robber barons were just following the capitalistic mandate of cutting costs and increasing profits by whatever means were allowable.

"Liberty produces wealth, wealth destroys liberty." Henry Demarest Lloyd, Wealth Against Commonwealth, 1894.

After decades of bloody union battles and protests, our government eventually reacted by establishing anti-trust laws and regulations of businesses (e.g., Standard Oil and Northern Securities were declared monopolies and broken up, the Federal Reserve was established, the Pure Food and Drug Act was passed, etc.)[173]. Progressive income taxes were instituted after a long fight, and help offset the "winner take all" aspect of our economic system.

Stocks and the financial markets were the next excess of capitalism. The excesses of an unregulated financial market and speculators led to the stock market crash of 1929 and the Great Depression. While Russia suffered through a revolution and communism, Franklin Roosevelt thwarted communism in the U.S. by giving us the New Deal to save capitalism from itself (giving us the SEC, FCC, FDIC, etc.). Some will argue World War II saved the economy, not the New Deal programs, but this was also a huge government intervention with deficit spending. The middle class was strengthened by job growth during World War II and a flood of qualified workers courtesy of the GI Bill providing free college education to veterans. Minimum wage laws, implemented since the end of the Great Depression, help lift people out of poverty and provide more consumers to drive our economy.[174] Henry Ford famously doubled the average worker wages in 1914, not only keeping his workers, but enabling his workers to afford his cars, creating a market.[175]

In recent decades, the middle class has been in decline again. This has been measured by both income and wealth. In 1944, the top 1% earned 11% of all U.S. income. By 2012, the take of the top 1% had doubled to 23%.[176] The top 3% had 44.8% of the wealth in 1989. By 2013, it had increased to 54.4%.[177] The gap throughout the world has increased, but the U.S. and Israel have the highest inequality. The richest 10% in the U.S. take home 16.5 times the income of the poorest 10%. In Israel, it is 15 times. The average for the 34 most developed countries is 9.6 times, and that is up from 7 times in the 1980s.[178]

The financial sector in particular has lobbied hard to exempt new financial gimmicks from regulation (eerily similar to the roaring 20s, which led to the Great Depression). Deregulation in general is good for the economy, but not if it turns into monopolies, large-scale fraud, and government bailouts. It is no coincidence that most of the recent rise in inequality between rich and poor is due to the new super-rich in the financial industry - America's top 25 hedge-fund managers make more than all the 500 CEOs of the S&P 500 combined.[179] The financial industry has generated artificial growth, simply reselling debt, such as mortgage loans which led to the 2008 crash (basically side bets causing fake growth of the economy). As a result, the financial industry has grown from 1-2% of GDP in 1970 to 9%.[180]

Various special interests have pushed independently for more regulation or subsidies in narrow areas, with no one looking out for the cumulative effect on small business and the middle class (which is supposed to be the job of Congress). Unions, which historically have looked out for workers, have had declining membership and influence.

The largest businesses in many industries, after multiple mergers, have succeeded in entrenching their profitable business models and basically stopping enforcement of the antitrust laws. As a result, due to enormous consolidation in many industries, Americans pay more for many services than other countries, resulting in an upward redistribution of wealth. We pay more for drugs than any other country, due to the consolidation of providers,[181] and the structure of our health system. Brand name drug makers have successfully lobbied to be able to pay generic makers to delay introducing cheaper generic drugs after patents on the branded drugs have expired. Internet connections are more expensive than in any other developed country because about 80 percent of users only have a single Internet service provider option. The U.S. went from nine major airline carriers in 2005 to only four in 2015, with many airports having only one or two, and US travel is thus more expensive than other countries.[182] In 2015, four food companies controlled 82 percent of beef packing and 85 percent of soybean processing.[183] Food prices have fallen around the world, while rising in the U.S.[184] The list goes on and on.

A study by the Economist magazine shows the consolidation has produced fat profits due to a lack of competition. Competition would normally lower prices, but that isn't happening. Rather than the money going to employees or being reinvested in equipment, etc., there are large amounts of cash simply being taken out of circulation. The Economist attributes part of this to a rise in lobbying the government over the last 10 years.[185] Thus one common denominator is campaign contributions and lobbying to prevent enforcement of antitrust laws.

Antitrust laws are not in the Constitution. They were enacted in response to the rise of the robber barons in the late 19th Century. They broadly prohibit monopolies and restraints of trade. But as recently interpreted by the Courts, when considering whether to approve a merger, the "beneficial effects" can be used to allow a merger that creates monopoly power. For example, the efficiencies of scale obtained are often argued to make the companies more competitive, and able to provide lower prices, benefiting consumers. The antitrust laws are enforced by the Department of Justice (DOJ) and the Federal Trade Commission (FTC). They are simply overwhelmed by the number of mergers and the hordes of private lawyers they have to fight. Other countries have modeled their antitrust laws on the pioneering U.S. laws. But other countries have improved on them, just as they have improved upon our Constitution. Many countries presume market dominance with anywhere from 20-50% market share, and thus place the burden on the companies to disprove this.

We are currently in an information revolution similar to the robber baron industrial revolution of the late 1800s. Companies are relentless in continuing to try to cut costs and improve profits.

Each year's profits need to increase over last year's profits to keep investors happy. Simply maintaining the same profits is not enough. Shipping jobs abroad and eliminating jobs due to automation originally targeted the lower level, clerical jobs. For example, in 2005 Blockbuster had 83,000 employees in the US. It has basically been replaced by Netflix, which employs just 2000 people.[186] Each year higher skill jobs are targeted. Currently, most white collar jobs are being targeted, including accountants, lawyers, technical writers, etc.[187] Companies are also using part-time employees, freelancers and independent contractors to take advantage of the government rules distinguishing employees from "independent contractors." This allows them to avoid the costs of employment laws, and to avoid paying medical insurance and other costs. Many new companies are adopting a business model with almost no employees, relying on independent contractors. Uber, Lyft and the other ride-share (private cab) companies do this, as do a host of app based companies: E.g., Instacart (grocery shopping), Washio (laundry), Spoonrocket (meal delivery), Handy (home cleaning and handyman), TaskRabbit (just about anything).[188] While employment has recovered from the 2008 recession, the jobs are paying less with fewer benefits, and many people have given up looking for work and thus aren't counted in the jobless statistics. The economy as a whole has grown, but the benefits of economic growth are skewed toward the rich.[189]

The combined effects of the inherent wealth concentration and special interest lobbying needs to be offset or we'll run out of consumers (the squeezed and laid-off workers) and the whole system will decline and eventually collapse.

The new aristocracy.
The United States was founded on the ideal of equality of opportunity– a meritocracy instead of the aristocracies of Europe. The meritocracy created by our Founders is gone. We don't have royalty, but we have its practical equivalent– a monied aristocracy. Some saw it coming early on.

> *"I hope we shall crush in its birth the aristocracy of our monied corporations which dare already to challenge our government to a trial by strength, and bid defiance to the laws of our country."* - Thomas Jefferson

In feudal times, nobles were given or seized land and power, which was handed down to the children of the nobility. In the U.S., fortunes are made with hard work, but also with government assistance– railroad land grants, oil leases, government contracts, laws which favor corporations, etc. For example, Carnegie, Vanderbilt and Rockefeller used government railroad land grants to build their fortunes. More recently, public airwaves were sold cheaply to enable monopolistic media fortunes to be built. Timber, mining, oil and other fortunes have been made with cheap leases of public land. The special benefits obtained by lobbying for the financial industry, defense contractors and other groups, as described above, has created more fortunes. Those fortunes are then passed down through generations, giving the advantages of capital as a birthright to the privileged few. This system is much less insidious than the feudal system, since in most cases the fortunes were at least partially earned in the first instance. However, the resulting disparity and unfairness for future generations is the same– people are awarded fortunes as a birthright, without earning it.

Recap.

We are currently seeing a perfect storm with both economic and political upheavals concentrating wealth and power. We are seeing more and more automation and increases in the gap between rich and poor. We have seen a drastic consolidation of the media and a transformation from being a political watchdog to being an entertainment and profit center. This has been aided and abetted by an unprecedented amount of special interest influence on the government through recent gaming of our political system. Most of the political changes described above have arisen in the last 50 years:

Primary elections– less than 20 states used these before 1968. The New Hampshire primary used to be in March in 1972, and has been moved up over the years to its current time in January to stay ahead of other states moving up their primary dates.

Sophisticated Gerrymandering– this has been an issue for a long time, but has been taken to unprecedented levels (99% of incumbents reelected) since the 1990s with the availability of mapping software and block-by-block census data.[190]

Huge campaign sums– this is largely driven by the cost of TV ads– the 1st televised debate was 1960. In 1974 it cost $53,000 to run for a seat in the House, but increased to $1.3 million by 2012.

Senate holds on bills– these have been around a long time, but expanded dramatically in the 80's.

Executive orders– These were rarely used until Reagan's administration in the 80s.

Signing statements– These were only ceremonial until Reagan in the 80s.

Complexity of Bills– The average length of a bill increased from 2 ½ pages in 1948 to 20 pages in 2013 (average lowered by simple building-naming bills).

States & Cities tax breaks to attract companies – This really started in 1985 with the bidding for GM's Saturn plant.

Deficit spending– Until the 1980s, this was confined to wars and other emergencies, such as the Great Depression. As of 2016, the total US debt was over $19 trillion (in 1980 it was under $1 trillion).

Congressional staff– the staff was cut by 20% since 1979, leaving Congress dependent on lobbyists for expertise.

Transparency– after the 1973 Watergate scandal, cameras and more transparency has made it difficult for Congress to compromise by giving up some ground.

Committees– reforms since the 1970s have transferred power to the partisan party leaders.

Earmarks– these were banned in 2011, eliminating a tool for compromise.

In spite of all the problems in our political system, there is not only an inability to change them by Congress, there is a hesitancy among the population to change how our government works. The government may not work well, but it is familiar and we are accustomed to its idiosyncrasies and afraid of change. But

Houston, we have a problem. Our Founders created a delicate balance, but left the implementation details to be supplied by Congress. That delicate balance has been upended.

So where does that leave us? The U.S. Constitution checks and balances, designed to avoid concentrated power, is borderline guaranteed to produce gridlock. The Constitution provided supermajority voting only for a few situations (2/3 for impeachment, expelling a member, overriding a veto and approving a treaty). A series of additional roadblocks has been added to the original checks and balances– the filibuster, holds on bills, unrelated amendments, signing statements and executive orders. Special interests fund campaigns and then lobby, using the roadblocks, to get what they want and punish politicians that don't comply, using negative ads. This special interest control is consolidated with an election process that allows radicals (beholden to special interests) to control candidates in primaries, then the elected incumbents gerrymander district boundaries to make their seats secure. With their stashes of money, and a weakened media beholden to their ad dollars, special interests are able to manipulate us voters to support their causes and make us think they are aligned with our interests. The political playing field is no longer level. The checks and balances are out of tune.

The Founders threw off rule by kings and nobles, and would be turning in their graves to see it replaced by a new aristocracy of special interests, with everyone else being squeezed. There is an adage that a frog will jump out if placed in boiling water, but if placed in cool water that is slowly heated to boiling, the frog won't note the gradual change and will eventually be boiled to death. Our system of government has evolved to boiling over 200 years for us frogs (with most of the heat increase in the last 50 years).

Are we going to let all the sacrifice of blood and sweat of earlier generations over 200 years go to waste? Will we be the generation that allows government of the people, by the people and for the people to perish from this earth?

VI. The Solution

WAITING FOR CONGRESS to act is a non-starter. Congress was elected under the current system of special interest control, and they owe their jobs to special interests. The Senators enjoy the power they have to act like each one is the President, with holds, riders and the filibuster. They are not going to change the system that got them there. Even if they wanted to, the special interests wouldn't let them. They will make grand promises to get elected, but will be hamstrung by the system and we'll continue to see watered-down laws riddled with exceptions for special interests.

We have a lot of good people trying their best in government, but we have put them in a system that forces them to kowtow to special interests, and subjects them to ridicule by the media. We need to help our employees– our representatives - do their job. We need a bold, comprehensive fix. The time for half measures and talk has passed.

There are multiple, intertwined problems as discussed above. There is no silver bullet to solve these problems– we need a package of solutions. The solutions are obvious. In fact, many groups have been working on them for decades. Many of these problems can be solved at the state level or in Congress. In fact, there have been some limited successes, such as redistricting reform in a handful of states. But they have been thwarted by the special interest controlled system. A piece-meal approach working within the system will take a long, long time, and likely will not succeed in many areas. We need a mechanism for a comprehensive solution. We need a way to change the system. That actually *is* in the Constitution.

There is a tool in the Constitution itself that has been gathering dust for over 200 years and has never been used. Every amendment to the Constitution has been proposed by Congress, and Congress won't act. But there is another way to amend the Constitution that our Founders wrote into the Constitution, anticipating exactly the situation we have now where Congress is the problem. The states themselves can call a Constitutional Convention. There is a provision for 2/3 of the states (34 states) to call a convention to amend the Constitution. Jefferson thought this should happen every generation, and Washington, Adams and Madison all encouraged future generations to amend the Constitution. We never have called such a convention. Now is the time, because Congress is the problem. So we need the states to fix it. We need to give the Constitution a long-overdue procedural tune-up.

There have been many proposals for a Constitutional Convention before, but we've never had one. In the 1800s the selection of senators by state legislatures had led to corruption with smoke-filled room selections. Since Congress wouldn't act, the states used the option provided by the Founders in the Constitution for just such a situation. They started a campaign for a constitutional convention to consider direct election of senators in the early 1900s. When the number of states calling for a convention approached the necessary 2/3, Congress proposed the 17th amendment for the direct election of senators to avoid a convention. It was approved by the states in 1913.

In the 1970s and 1980s, many states pushed for a balanced budget amendment, but fell short of the required 34 states. More than 34 states have passed such proposals, but 17 subsequently rescinded, with some of those re-passing as the legislatures have changed hands between the parties over the years. In a new push, as of March 2, 2016 six states had called for a Constitutional Convention to consider a balanced budget amendment and other amendments to impose fiscal restraints on the federal government (somewhat of a return to the Articles of Confederation).[191] In 2011, progressive Harvard Law School Professor Lawrence Lessig with co-chair, Mark Meckler, co-founder of the Tea Party Patriots, organized ConConCon, a Conference to consider a Constitutional Convention linking campaign finance reform and federal budget limits. They were unable to agree.[192] But this was the right idea– a basic compromise of giving the conservatives the balanced budget they want and giving the liberals the campaign finance reform they want.

The special interests oppose a Constitutional Convention– they want to protect their turf. The special interests have shot this down before with the fear of a runaway convention. If this idea gains traction, the special interests will say the convention could rewrite the Second Amendment and make gun ownership illegal, ban abortion, make Islam the official religion, force us all to watch Star Trek re-runs every night, etc. But this is hogwash for two reasons. First, the states can limit the subjects to be addressed at the Convention. Many will point out that this was tried at our original Constitutional Convention, which was supposed to just amend the Articles of Confederation, and that didn't work. But that convention met in secret. With the media coverage and public pressure we'd have today, that is highly unlikely. In addition, the second reason is that not only are 2/3 of the states required to call a convention, an even higher percentage, ¾ of the states (38 states), need to approve any amendments. Thus, just 13 states can block it. There is no way ¾ of the states are going to approve such out of scope amendments. In any event, if 38 states can actually agree on something, perhaps we should do it. It will also be pointed out that the Articles of Confederation required a unanimous vote for amendments, and the Founders changed that so the Constitution would be adopted when 9 of 13 colonies approved. However, that was when there was a weak federal government, which was the whole reason for the Constitutional Convention. The federal government is much, much stronger now, and fought a civil war over an attempt to form a new government outside the Constitution. It simply isn't going to happen again.

Ideally, convention delegates would act in a non-partisan manner, rather than having the existing parties try to maintain a perceived advantage under different aspects of the current system. But a convention can't be isolated from politics. There is a legitimate fear of Republicans trying to rewrite the Constitution to their advantage. Delegates would be appointed by the states, and Republicans in 2016 controlled both houses of 30 state legislatures. But this is likely a high-water mark– they have already squeezed the maximum out of Gerrymandering. Demographic shifts will reduce this advantage over time. Thus, it is still 8 short of the number of states needed to approve any amendments and highly unlikely to go higher.

There is also a fear that special interests will control the convention. But delegates do not need to raise campaign dollars, and are not running for re-election, so they are not very susceptible to influence. The state legislators who will appoint them, however, are subject to such influence. But since this is one step removed, it should be difficult to control the delegates. In any event, the ultimate protection is the requirement that both Democrat and Republican states approve the resulting amendments. There is simply no risk free way to fix the system – we need to trust the tool the Founders gave us and take a leap of faith.

The delegates could draw on experts in each subject matter area, to assist with the details and understanding the pros and cons of alternatives. The convention could be limited to the following subject matter, but could come up with different solutions. By focusing on the mechanics of elections and governing, and not divisive substantive issues, such a convention will have a shot at success. The proposals below should be obvious now that the problems are understood. Perhaps some of the proposals below aren't the best way to deal with the problem. But we should get our best and brightest in a room to figure that out. To have a chance at getting sufficient state support, the convention should stay away from controversial, substantive issues, such as gun control, abortion, etc. The convention should also stay away from any change to the states relative voting power in the federal government since that would doom obtaining approval of ¾ of the states.

Parliamentary system, single body of Congress.

Having Congress elect the President would eliminate many of the gridlock problems caused by divided government. But that is just not going to happen– the American people are too wedded to and comfortable with the current system– or rather too afraid of such a dramatic change. Likewise, a single body of Congress, rather than a House and Senate, would cut down on gridlock. But there is no way the smaller states would approve such a change unless it was just the Senate, with equal representation for each state. There is no way the large states would agree to give up their numbers in the House, so this is a non-starter (plus the Constitution specifically prohibits amendments to the equal representation in the Senate). Some things haven't changed in 200 years. But there are things we can do, that have been proposed with wide support.

Proposed subjects for a constitutional convention:

1.   Campaign finance reform.

Campaign finance is the number one problem. Special interests literally buy our representatives. We force our representatives to go hat-in-hand to special interests for campaign expense money.

The country is littered with failed attempts to regulate campaign financing. In 1971, Congress passed the Federal Election Campaign Act, which required candidates to report expenses and contributions. After the Nixon Watergate scandal, the act was amended to limit individual contributions. The 2002 McCain-Feingold bill banned soft money contributions to national parties and restricted candidate-specific advertising by private interest groups. Lawyers found a way around the limits with "independent" Political Action Committees (PACs) which could spend on particular issues and attack an opponent rather than funneling money to a candidate.

But the Supreme Court has blown apart even these feeble regulations, in particular with the 2010 Citizens United decision. The Supreme Court said that spending is speech, since in today's world you can't get your political message out without money. Thus political spending is protected under the First Amendment guarantee of free speech.[193] We even subsidize this special interest spending, since much is done by nonprofits under sections 527 and 501(c) of the tax code.[194] The Citizens United case spawned "super PACs" that now do the negative advertising for candidates, allowing candidates to distance themselves from the really nasty attacks. Regulations to make the PACs independent won't solve the problem. No coordination is needed to figure out to air an attack ad against the opponent of the candidate you support.

The solution to special interests buying our representatives is obvious– let's outbid them. Instead of having our representatives on the payroll of corporations and unions, let's put them on *our* payroll for all of their expenses, so they really do work for us. Make them beholden to us (the voters) for the financing they need.

This can be done by providing for public financing of Congressional campaigns. Where public financing has been done (at local levels and in other countries) candidates are required to raise a qualifying amount themselves and/or get sufficient signatures, so only serious candidates get funding.[195] You may object to your hard-earned tax dollars going to someone you oppose. But guess what– it's already happening– special interests that you are opposed to are getting politicians to spend many orders of magnitude more of your tax dollars on causes you loath.

Many people have been convinced they are against public financing of campaigns because they think it is a waste of money that would raise our taxes to pay for the public funding (hmmm – perhaps a special interest manipulation of us?). But in fact common sense tells us that public financing would reduce our taxes. The cost of public financing would be about $7 billion (the amount spent on all federal campaigns [representatives, senators, President] in the 2012 campaigns).[196] It would be less in off years where there is no presidential election. Since there is only an election every other year, that is about $3.5 billion/year.

For comparison consider that, for example, if you're a Republican (at least not an old, poor Republican) you might object to the fact that we spend $498 billion a year on Medicare (including excessive, non-negotiable costs imposed on Medicare part D drug payments), $274 billion on Medicaid (health insurance for the poor) and $398 billion a year on safety net programs, such as the earned income tax credit, food stamps, low income housing, etc. (See Appendix III). If you're a Democrat,

96

you may object to 95% of the $77 billion yearly lower tax on capital gains compared to income tax) going to those earning $200,000 a year or more, or the top 5% in income getting 38% of the $183 billion/year for mortgage interest deductions, imputed interest exclusions and capital gains exclusions for homeowners. Whether you are a Republican or a Democrat, you probably resent corporate subsidies and off-shore tax havens that cost $284 billion a year. With public funding Congress wouldn't be beholden to special interests and wouldn't be granting these subsidies. At a minimum, public funding would pay for itself many times over and would drastically reduce the amount of your dollars going to things you oppose.

This doesn't even count indirect costs of not having public funding. The financial sector special interests caused us to lose a lot of money and jobs by collapsing the economy in 2008 with shaky mortgage schemes. These schemes were made possible by campaign contributions and lobbying against government regulation. It doesn't count the money government influence cost us (with higher prices than in other countries) by stifling competition and thwarting enforcement of antitrust laws. This results in our paying higher prices, compared to other countries, for drugs, airline tickets, internet, etc.

If Congress hadn't needed campaign contributions from the financial industry, would they have allowed unregulated derivative trading and other practices that ended up tanking the economy and requiring the taxpayers to bail out Wall Street? If money from the health industry wasn't needed, the originally proposed cost controls of Obamacare could have been implemented, saving us hundreds of billions of dollars in health costs. There are many more examples.

A possible objection is that this would give incumbents an advantage. But incumbents already have a huge advantage. That advantage is largely taken away if the challenger gets the same amount of money, and the incumbent can't dispense favors to raise money. Studies of states with public funding found a decline in the number of races where incumbents were unopposed.[197] Also, eliminating gerrymandering will reduce the incumbent advantage.

97

Many other countries and some US states provide for public funding of political campaigns. Currently, the US only provides matching funds, and only for the presidential candidates (which are sometimes turned down to avoid the limits placed on total spending).[198]

In one proposed solution, candidates who qualify for public funding (enough signatures and seed donations) should get free or low cost TV time to limit the cost to taxpayers. Most of the money spent by politicians is for TV advertising. A condition of the government grants to media companies of public airwave frequencies should be low cost ads during election campaigns.[199] In addition, there should be disclosures of who is doing independent political spending, limiting duration of campaigning to limit costs (e.g., no early primaries), and requiring reduced rates for TV and other advertising. This is not a new idea. Public financing is supported by many groups[200] and a Gallup poll in 2013 found half of Americans support it.[201]

While public financing takes away the special interest carrot, it doesn't take away their stick of negative ads. To counter such negative attack ads which threaten representatives, public financing can include a fund to provide qualifying candidates, and sitting representatives, money to counteract independent attack ads. It could be called the "we have your back" fund– for having the back of our representatives that do the right thing (an even if they are doing the wrong thing, they should have an opportunity to explain). At a minimum, funding up to a limit could be provided, and after that, to limit public costs, require the funder of the attack ads to fund equal time for the opposite view.

This is also not a new idea. Arizona and others provided trigger funds– additional public grants made available to a publicly funded candidate facing high opposition spending. In June 2011, the U.S. Supreme Court (*Arizona Free Enterprise Club v. Bennett*) declared that Arizona's trigger funds were unconstitutional (they burdened the First Amendment rights of those who opposed publicly funded candidates). Thus, this aspect needs to be constitutionally addressed.

If candidates win our elections, they should be provided the tools (funds) to carry out what we elected them to do, without being intimidated by special interest threats of attack ads. If we put them in the line of fire, to defend us, we should provide them with ammo.

2. Independent commission to set congressional district boundaries.

The Constitution currently gives the authority to set district boundaries to the incumbent state legislature. The legislatures are currently gerrymandering district boundaries and thus picking their own voters to stay in power. 90% of all districts are now safe for the incumbent party. This is clearly a flawed system. We should instead require independent commissions to set boundaries, as has been done in a number of states (California, Arizona, Hawaii, Idaho, Montana, New Jersey and Washington). A number of other states have independent commissions for their state legislatures, but not for their congressional delegations.[202] In June of 2015 the Supreme Court narrowly (5-4) upheld the ability of these states to transfer this power from the legislature to an independent commission.[203] The Constitution should be amended to set up an independent federal commission to set boundaries, perhaps except in states that have already done this (and the independence and the boundaries must pass muster with guidelines of the federal commission).[204]

3. Establish uniform voting requirements and rules.

Each state currently makes its own rules, and both Republicans and Democrats try to reduce voter turnout for different elections. This reduces the voting power of the average citizen compared to those most easily manipulated by special interests. Uniform rules should be established, such as weekend voting, automatic voter registration upon obtaining a driver's license, uniform standards on the identification required, more early and absentee voting, and requiring local elections be the same day.

4. Prohibit congressional voting procedures that defeat constitutional balance.

Filibusters, holds and Christmas tree bills add extra supermajorities or mechanisms to defeat bills beyond those set forth in the Constitution. This gives special interests a way to block laws, or enact laws that the majority do not support, and lead to gridlock with the numbers skyrocketing in recent years. The Founders did not foresee this upending of the Constitutional intent by Congress. The rules aren't in the Constitution, but some basics should be. In particular, rules that defeat the balance set forth in the Constitution should be prohibited. For example, end or reform the Filibuster,[205] eliminate unrelated amendments/riders (except earmarks for state infrastructure & other state projects) and end holds. Perhaps, to avoid any future new tricks, require that a bill with sufficient support can be brought to a vote in a reasonable time (e.g., 40-50% of the members can sign a petition to force a vote).

5. Lobbyists can't hire ex members of Congress for 5 years.

Fifty percent of members of Congress become lobbyists, with an average pay increase of 1452%. Clearly, this provides motivation for giveaways to special interests. Limits should be imposed on members of Congress and their staff so they can't work as lobbyists for 5 years after leaving office. This will reduce representatives and senators pandering to special interests in order to get a better paying job. There is a current law prohibiting senators and executive officials from becoming registered lobbyists for 2 years after leaving government, and 1 year for representatives. But it is clearly too short as can be seen from the numbers becoming lobbyists, and the amount of money thrown at them. Also, it doesn't prevent them from working for lobbying firms, just not being a registered lobbyist.[206]

6. Lengthen House terms.

Representatives are constantly running for office, and start fundraising anew for their next term the first day on the job. They have to constantly appeal to voters who are informed by sound bites and don't appreciate the complex trade-offs of legislation. This is an example of too much direct democracy setting the stage for special interest manipulation of us to get what they want from representatives. Public funding of campaigns may reduce the need for this, but we need to be sure. Some voters think they are keeping their representatives on a short leash, but we voters are too subject to manipulation by special interests– voters with the opposite views of you, of course. The constant campaigning causes representatives to be constantly posturing for voters, making them unwilling to compromise to get things done.

Our representatives need to be more isolated from us, like the Senate. We should change the House terms from the current 2 years to 4 years so they aren't constantly running for office. The original Constitutional Convention considered 3 years before settling on 2, but that was before our current practice of starting campaigns 2 years ahead.

The Senate might also be addressed. The Senate has 6 year terms, with 1/3 elected every 2 years. Thus, half are in non-presidential election years, with lower voter turnout and interest, which leads to divided government. One option is to change the senate term to 8 years, with re-election every 4 years, to align with presidential elections. This will hopefully provide less divided government, with the shorter reelection term limiting the incumbent advantage. This will address the permanent campaign, if combined with a reform of the primary system.[207] In any event, we should get some smart people in a room to figure out if we can eliminate off-year elections– we voters don't pay enough attention and are too easily manipulated. It will also reduce the costs of public financing of campaigns.

7.   Require accrual accounting and a balanced budget.

The total US debt increased from $3 trillion in 1990 to over $19 trillion in 2016, and that doesn't count another $63.5 trillion in unfunded Medicare, Social Security and federal pension benefits. Accounting firms have noted that the lack of accrual accounting creates an incentive for elected officials to curry favor with today's voters at the expense of tomorrow's taxpayers. As a result, huge future obligations are incurred and hidden.

We need to address this. Now. We need the flexibility to deficit spend to address recessions, so a yearly balanced budget doesn't make fiscal sense and would be economic suicide for the country. If a yearly balanced budget was required, we would have lost World War II, which required a huge amount of deficit spending with war bonds. The Great Depression might never have ended. In a recession, tax revenues are down and unemployment claims are up. Requiring a balanced budget in a recession would make it worse– pulling money out of the economy and leading to a downward spiral. Also, some amount of debt is reasonable and healthy, but not the levels we have now.

However, we should at least require that the budget each year should show how it can be eventually balanced over a business cycle (show balance over period of years). Alternately, balancing over a business cycle can be required, with appropriate exceptions for emergencies, and giving the President a line item veto over appropriations. This has been done with success in Sweden.[208] Some countries, such as New Zealand and Australia, have adopted accrual accounting for government. We need to limit the natural tendency to pander to current voters/special interests by passing the bill to future generations.

8. Reform primary process.

Our current primary process leads to radicals being nominated and provides an avenue for special interest control. We need to consider different options to reform the primary process. Open primaries is one reform that counters the polarization of our parties. An open primary allows Republicans to vote in Democratic primaries and vice-versa. Currently, few people vote in primaries, and those that do tend to be the most partisan. Thus, they decide the candidate, and in a gerrymandered, safe district, they decide the winner of the general election. Open primaries force candidates to appeal to a broad range of voters, and thus be less fanatically partisan.

Another option is having all the primaries on the same day, or within a short period of time, and limiting how early they begin. This would eliminate the undue influence of some states, and shorten the campaign season. This would also reduce the amount of money needed and allow representatives to focus on representing us, not campaigning, for most of their time in office.

Another proposed solution is instant runoff elections, which are used in many other countries. Basically, the primary election and the general election are combined into a single election. Voters only have to show up once, and they vote for their first and second choices. This would shorten the campaign season as well. Alternately, the primary can narrow the field, still leaving more than one choice from each major party for the general election. There are also a variety of proposals for random assignment of primary dates, having smaller states first but a more compressed timeframe and regional primaries.[209]

9. Multi-representative districts.

Our winner take all system leaves large numbers of voters without representation. A state that is 40% Republican and has 10 representatives, even without gerrymandering, will currently have 10 Democrats representing it. It would be fairer to have 6 Democrats and 4 Republicans. Most of the original states had at-large or multi-representative districts, which assured the minority in a district would have some representation. Today we have a winner-take-all system that leaves a minority without representation (a minority that is often nearly half the population, or, with gerrymandering, is actually a majority). This can be addressed by having larger districts, with multiple representatives for each district. This could be combined with preferential or cumulative voting (voters have multiple votes for the multiple seats, with 1st, 2nd, etc. choices), so the majority party doesn't just get all the seats.

10. Supreme Court– 18 year term, standing for Congress-President disputes.

With the life expectancy at the time of the adoption of Constitution, a lifetime appointment of a judge meant a 40 year old appointed as a judge would serve for about 15 years. With today's life expectancies, a 40 year old would serve an average of 40 years. We currently have lifetime appointments of young judges to the Supreme Court to extend the years of influence, and accordingly intense fighting in the Senate over confirmation. A number of people have proposed that instead, each justice should be appointed for an 18 year term. These could be staggered, so that each president can nominate 2, eliminating the current gamesmanship.[210] A similar term can be provided for other federal judges.

The Constitution requirement of the "advice and consent" of the Senate provides no mechanism for resolving standoffs. The standoffs have escalated, with the Senate refusing to consider any nominee by President Obama. With the new 18 year staggered terms, we could flip the current process where a filibuster can block a nominee, and instead require a 60% vote to reject a nominee. That should provide sufficient protection against clearly unqualified nominees.

The Supreme Court assumed, and ad-hoc developed, the role of referee, deciding what laws are constitutional. We should build in a thought-out process for this. In particular, currently the Supreme Court won't hear a case for years, and not at all if someone doesn't have standing to sue (be personally affected). Instead, Congress or the President should be able to appeal directly and immediately to the Supreme Court to make a call, like a referee. Standing should be provided for Congress to request review of executive orders and signing statements, and any other action Congress believes intrudes on its jurisdiction. The President should be granted standing to request review of laws believed unconstitutional and any Legislative vetoes (or other areas where Congress is believed to be intruding on the administrative areas of the President).

11. No congressional agencies and independent commission to decide which companies get government contracts.

Congress, in its grab for power, has created agencies that report to it, instead of the president. Each committee, or even each senator, wants its own agency. Thus, we have competing agencies. This has led to mind-boggling bureaucracy. Instead, any created agencies should report to the President as contemplated by the separation of powers in the Constitution, or be independent. This will avoid encroachment on the powers of the President and corresponding retaliatory actions by the President to reclaim power, and also help reduce the number of overlapping agencies (since each senator can't have his/her own agency).

Every state wants government contracts for its businesses, and will fight to maintain them against the interests of the country as a whole. While smaller projects can be useful as earmarks to enable compromise, larger projects across multiple states can get out of hand. A model for solving the state competition problem was the successful commission to decide which military bases should be closed (to get around the Congressional gridlock due to no state wanting its bases closed).[211] Congress could be required to establish a temporary independent commission to make these decisions. They would decide where military bases go and who gets huge government contracts, such as a new fleet of fighter planes. For smaller earmark projects, Congress can be limited to passing laws for new projects, but the President and the administration can choose the contractors without Congressional interference.

12. Prohibit federal, state and local tax breaks to individual businesses or industries.

States have recently competed in giving out tax breaks to attract businesses. This is a race to the bottom, hurting their tax bases. States and local jurisdictions need to be saved from themselves. The Federal Government also gives special tax breaks to lobbying special interests, rather than just giving them money, because it is easier to hide. Tax breaks should not be allowed for individual businesses or industries at any level. If there is a true need, and the government wants to subsidize an industry, it should do so through a direct subsidy, which is more visible to voters.

13. Judge trials, not jury trials, for patent and antitrust cases.

Using ordinary jurors for complex patent and antitrust cases drives up the costs and provides arbitrary results. These cases should be tried by judges or masters who are experienced in the technology or antitrust laws. Consideration can also be given to whether we want to end the right to jury trials for other lawsuits between companies, preserving the right to a jury trial for criminal cases and cases with a person as a party.

14. Term limits.

It isn't clear that term limits would be effective, since the states that have adopted them appear to have had mixed success – some downsides are a loss of experience and more short-term thinking instead of long-term planning.[212] The other reforms discussed above should also reduce any need for term limits. We have presidential term limits (two terms), and a proposal above for Supreme Court term limits to 18 years. However, something less than a lifetime in Congress may be appropriate, but long enough to allow the benefits of experience. Currently, the

Supreme Court has held that term limits for Congress would be unconstitutional, so this would require a Constitutional amendment.[213]

15. Measures to facilitate compromise.

There are a number of rule changes that can facilitate compromise. They should probably not be enshrined in a difficult to amend Constitution in case there are unforeseen consequences and change is needed. But leaving it to Congress to adopt reasonable rules hasn't worked. Perhaps these provisions can require a lower threshold for amendment, such as 55% of Congress and 55% of the states. There are three main features commentators have suggested to improve the atmosphere for compromise and getting things done in Congress. (1) Transparency could be limited to testimony, and privacy allowed for sensitive negotiations and compromise. (2) Committees' could have their authority restored, and members could be randomly assigned to prevent a concentration that favors a particular policy.[214] (3) Earmarks can be allowed with restrictions, such as a maximum dollar amount, requiring the sponsor to be identified, and not making a particular special interest as a beneficiary.[215]

Another issue that has been discussed is the size of the House. At 435 members, the House appears too big for the members to get to know each other and work together to compromise. A smaller House would seem likely to encourage compromise, although some commentators argue for a much larger House to provide more direct democracy. One problem with changing the size of the House is that it will affect the voting power of the states. Each state currently gets 2 Electoral College votes, plus a vote for each representative. Lowering the number of representatives would increase the relative voting power of smaller states, while increasing the number of representatives would increase the relative voting power of larger states (since larger numbers would make the two vote per state allocation a smaller portion of the total). Thus, one group of states would protest either way. One solution is to keep the electoral votes the same, while changing the number of representatives, or even weighting the votes of representatives to maintain the current voting power with fewer representatives.

Conclusion

OUR POLITICAL SYSTEM has broken down. The tide moving to direct democracy has had the unintended consequence of making things worse– decisions are made by the uninformed, polarized and manipulated masses– us. We need to do what the Founders would have done: level the playing field by restoring the checks and balances to protect us. But it won't happen unless we the people demand it. The world is watching. Will the U.S. step up and fix the system? Or will other countries turn to China's example of authoritarian state-run capitalism? The gauntlet has been thrown down. Will we pick it up?

Objections will come from all quarters. The rich and special interests won't want to give up campaign financing influence. Liberals won't want limits on spending with a budget and accrual accounting. But therein lies the basis of a grand bargain. The other proposals end advantages that both parties have taken advantage of. While the Republicans have taken more advantage of gerrymandering, that will surely change in the future due to demographic changes. The party in the minority won't want to give up the filibuster and other tricks. Each party won't want to give up Gerrymandering in states where it is to their advantage. But everyone needs to give up their short-term advantage for their long-term advantage and the long term health of the country. No one wins in the long run if we continue our current course, and bankrupt the country or cause a revolution.

What you can do for your country.
Start or sign a petition on Change.org or a similar platform. An example is in Appendix I. Write or call your state representative. Write a letter to the editor. Organize a protest. Use your imagination. Do something.

"Ask not what your country can do for you, ask what you can do for your country." John F. Kennedy, Inaugural Address, Jan. 20, 1961.

APPENDIX I

PETITION

To: Legislature of the State of _____.

Please vote for a limited constitutional convention to address the undue influence of special interests on the government and enable Congress to function (e.g., campaign finance, federal budget, setting Congressional district boundaries, and to give the Constitution a procedural tune-up on the issues identified in Common Cents).

APPENDIX II

The state of _____ hereby asks Congress to call a U.S. Constitutional Convention as provided in Article V of the U.S. Constitution. The convention shall be limited to the following topics or related provisions to tune-up the Constitution to limit special interest influence and improve the operation of government:

    A. **Campaign finance, election and Congressional voting reform**.
    1.   Public funding of campaigns.
    2.   Drawing Congressional district boundaries.
    3.   Senate and House voting procedures.
    4.   Reform primary elections.
    5.   Multi-representative districts.
    6.   Uniform voting rules.
    B. **House and Court terms, court standing**.
    7.   Terms of House Representatives.
    8.   Supreme Court terms and Congress/President disputes standing.
    9.   Term limits.
    C. **Accrual Budget**
    10. Budget and accrual accounting.
    D. **Limits on tax breaks, lobbying, congressional agencies and jury trial for patent & antitrust**.
    11. Limit lobbyist hiring of members of Congress.
    12. Independent commission for government contracts, no Congressional agencies.

13.   No tax breaks to individual businesses or sectors.

14.   Judge trial, not jury trial, for patent, antitrust cases.

E.   **Measures to encourage compromise**

15.   Allow earmarks, private negotiations and change committee assignments.

APPENDIX III

BUDGET, TAX NUMBERS
Major US budget categories[216]

Below are the top 6 US federal budget categories, accounting for 83% of the budget. The biggest benefits go to everyone, but the poor get the most. Also benefited in a big way are the weapons and health insurance industries.

Category	Percent of budget	Who benefits
Social Security - $814 billion	24%	Every worker [amount of income taxed is capped to match the high end of benefits]
Defense - $643 billion	19%	Everyone (security), military contractors.[217]
Medicare - $498 billion	14%	Everyone, health insurance companies [note rich subsidize poor – level of income taxed not capped, rich tend to use less, perhaps offset by longer lives].
safety net programs, such as the earned income tax credit, food stamps, low income housing, etc. - $398 billion	12%	Poor.
Medicaid (health insurance	8%	Poor.

for the poor) - $274 billion		
Interest on national debt - $221 billion	6 %	Everyone

To determine whom the government favors, we can mainly look to who pays taxes and who/what gets a pass on taxes.

<u>Top 10 Deductions.</u>[218]
The rich get most of tax benefits, but also pay a higher rate & more dollars. However, keep in mind that every dollar lost due to a deduction means higher taxes for everyone else. It is a backdoor method to lower the rate for just those who can take advantage of the deductions. Also note that this just deals with Federal Income taxes. Sales and other taxes take a higher percentage of lower incomes, such that we essentially have an overall flat tax in the US.

Category	Amount/year	Who benefits
Health insurance contributions	$184 billion	Insurance companies & those lucky enough to work for companies that provide health insurance.
Mortgage interest deductions	$98 billion	38% of the dollars go to those in the top 5% of income[219]
Capital gains and dividends lower rate (15%)	$77 billion	95% goes to those making over $200,000 per year[220]
Tax free Retirement plan contributions	$67 billion	36% goes to top 5% in income
Step-up in basis to reduce capital gains tax to heirs	$61 billion	
Exclusion of	$50 billion	38% goes to top

imputed interest for home owners		5% in income
Deductions of state and local taxes	$48 billion	90% goes to those making over $100,000[221]
Non 401K, IRA retirement plan deductions	$45 billion	36% goes to top 5%
Charitable contributions	$43 billion	59% goes to top 5% in income
Capital gains exclusion on home sales	$35 billion	Likely same as mortgage interest - 38% goes to top 5% of income

Major subsidies, loopholes:

Off-shore tax havens - $184 billion/yr.[222]

Corporate subsidies - $100 billion/yr.[223]

Estate tax under Bush v. under Clinton - $40 billion/yr.[224]

Taxes not collected due to $2 billion in cuts to IRS budget between 2010 and 2014[225] - $12 billion.

Examples of targeted tax benefits due to lobbying[226]:

Three-year depreciation for racehorses.

Credit for railroad track maintenance.

Mine rescue team training credit.

Election to expense advanced mine safety equipment.

Enhanced charitable deduction for contributions of food inventory.

Accelerated depreciation for business property on Indian reservation.

Exceptions for certain foreign income for banking & insurance businesses.

Rebate of excises taxes on rum distilled in Puerto Rico and U.S. Virgin Islands.

7-year recovery period for motorsports entertainment complexes.

A variety of deductions for oil & gas drilling.[227]

Crop insurance subsidies (majority to rich, corporate farmers).[228]

Indian country coal production tax credit.

There are many others, some seeming worthwhile, such as credits for different types of renewable energy, although some energy credits are suspect.

<u>Indirect subsidies – Laws & regulations that provide financial advantages to certain industries & special interests.</u>

Lobbyists tout the return on investment from lobbying, in the form of targeted tax benefits (return is 6x - 21x), more generous depreciation treatment, and a lower hazard rate of being detected for fraud.[229] Here are just some examples:

- Food pyramid modified from proposed "eat less red meat" to "eat more lean meat" and meaningless color coded triangle. Benefits cattle industry.

- Large banks can borrow money at a lower rate than small banks, because creditors assume the federal government will rescue them. This provides an annual $83 billion advantage.[230]

- Federal aid, loans to colleges (including for profit colleges whose graduates don't have the skills to get jobs).[231]

- Car seats mandated for older children where seat belts are just as effective.[232]

- Teacher lobbies keep even incompetent teachers from being fired, stop good teachers from being paid for performance, and lock in unsustainable pension benefits.[233]

Bibliography

Books

"Imperfect Union: The Constitutional Roots of the Mess We're In," Eric Black (Jan. 14, 2013).

"Political Order and Political Decay : From the Industrial Revolution to the Globalization of Democracy" Francis Fukuyama (2014).

"Unequal Democracy, The Political Economy of the New Gilded Age," Larry M. Bartels (2010).

"The Assault on Reason," Al Gore (2007).

"America's Bitter Pill: Money, Politics, Backroom Deals, and the Fight to Fix Our Broken Healthcare System," Steven Brill (2015).

Caroline M. Hoxby, Our Schools, & Our Future, (2003)

"The Winner-Take-All Society: Why the Few at the Top Get So Much More Than the Rest of Us," Robert Frank and Philip Cook (Penguin Books, 1996)

"The Bully Pulpit," Doris Kearns Goodwin (Simon & Schuster, 2013).

Websites

public financing of campaigns:

http://www.commoncause.org/issues/money-in-politics/

http://ofby.us/

http://lwv.org/issues/reforming-money-politics

Redistricting (end gerrymandering):

http://www.commoncause.org/states/california/issues/voting-and-elections/redistricting/what-is-redistricting-reform.html

http://redistricting.lls.edu/reform.php

http://www.endgerrymandering.com/

Senate Filibuster, rules:

http://fixthesenatenow.org

Reform primary elections:

http://fixtheprimaries.com/

Voting reform, ranked choice voting:

http://www.fairvote.org/

http://www.cfer.org/

Term limits:

https://www.termlimits.org/

Supreme Court terms:

http://fixthecourt.com/the-fixes/

Balanced Budget:

http://www.balanceourbudget.com/

Lobbying:

http://www.cleanupwashington.org/lobbying/page.cfm?pagei
d=46

http://sunlightfoundation.com/policy/lobbying/

Measures to encourage compromise

http://hewlett.org/programs/special-projects/madison-
initiative

Endnotes

[1] "Strong Majority of Americans, NRA Members Back Gun Control," Seth Cline, US News and World Report (Jan. 28, 2013): http://www.usnews.com/news/articles/2013/01/28/strong-majority-of-americans-nra-members-back-gun-control

[2] Most of the lawsuits under the California Environmental Quality Act have been NIMBY (Not In My Back Yard) suits targeting urban infill projects and transit projects, not urban sprawl, driving up the cost of housing. See "In the Name of the Environment: Litigation Abuse Under CEQA," Jennifer L. Hernandez, David Friedman, Stephanie M. DeHerrera (Aug. 2015): https://www.hklaw.com/publications/In-the-Name-of-the-Environment-Litigation-Abuse-Under-CEQA-August-2015/

[3] The Founders drew on precedent from England, with its House of Lords and House of Commons. They believed Congress would be the most powerful branch, and splitting it in two would be a check on that power (along with the Presidential veto).

[4] Eric Black, Imperfect Union: The Constitutional Roots of the Mess We're In, Kindle location 1603.

[5] Absent safeguards, a democracy may not remain a democracy. For example, Hugo Chavez did this to Venezuela. After taking office, he followed the President-as-dictator playbook of arresting the opposition, intimidating and taking over the media, nationalizing profitable companies and changing the constitution. He also provides cash benefits to the majority poor (many far left liberals would love this), but the giveaways were unsustainable and ruined the economy. There are many other examples of "democracies" in name only, with rigged elections, including Russia, Jordan, Thailand, Nigeria, Kenya and Bahrain. See "West 'embraces sham democracies,'" BBC News, Jan. 31, 2008: http://news.bbc.co.uk/2/hi/7219708.stm See also http://en.wikipedia.org/wiki/List_of_controversial_elections

[6] I wanted to include some of the pithy quotes you can find on the Internet, such as Thomas Jefferson equating democracy with mob rule. However, I was disappointed to find, upon investigation, that all my favorite quotes like this turned out to be false.

121

[7] U.S. Constitution, Article II, section 1, clause 3, as amended by Amendment XII: "The Electors shall meet in their respective states and vote by ballot for President and Vice-President, one of whom, at least, shall not be an inhabitant of the same state with themselves; ...."

[8] Originally the 5 top candidates, amended by the 12th amendment to the 3 top candidates: "and if no person have such majority, then from the persons having the highest numbers not exceeding three on the list of those voted for as President, the House of Representatives shall choose immediately, by ballot, the President."

[9] https://en.m.wikipedia.org/wiki/Electoral_College_(United_State s)

[10] Black, Imperfect Union, location 360.

[11] Instead, they use the Congressional District Method: the electoral votes are distributed based on the popular vote winner within each of the state's congressional districts, with the statewide popular vote winner receiving two additional electoral votes. See https://en.m.wikipedia.org/wiki/Electoral_College_(United_State s)

[12] See, for number of representatives: https://en.m.wikipedia.org/wiki/Current_members_of_the_United _States_House_of_Representatives; See for poll identifying party affiliation: http://www.gallup.com/poll/114016/state-states-political-party-affiliation.aspx

[13] "George Washington's Farewell Address 1796, ConstitutionFacts.com: http://www.constitutionfacts.com/us-founding-fathers/george-washingtons-farewell-address/

[14] The biggest impetus for civil service was thhttp://www.gallup.com/poll/114016/state-states-political-party-affiliation.aspxe assassination of President Garfield in 1881 by a disgruntled office seeker who didn't get the job he wanted under the patronage system. This led to the Civil Service Reform Act of 1883, dealing with patronage at the federal level. The civil service system includes protective rules to avoid arbitrary firing

of employees by newly elected politicians who want to hand out patronage to their supporters. An undesirable side effect, however, has been to make it harder to hold government employees accountable for doing quality work and fire ones that are incompetent.

[15] "States Ranked by Size & Population," ipL2 For Kids: http://www.ipl.org/div/stateknow/popchart.html

[16] The Iowa governor urged the defeat of Ted Cruz because he did not support the ethanol subsidy: "Iowa governor wants Ted Cruz defeated," MJ Lee, CNN Politics (Jan. 19, 2016): http://www.cnn.com/2016/01/19/politics/terry-branstad-ted-cruz-defeat/

[17] U.S. Constitution, Article 1, Section 4:
The Times, Places and Manner of holding Elections for Senators and Representatives, shall be prescribed in each State by the Legislature thereof; but the Congress may at any time by Law make or alter such Regulations, except as to the Places of chusing Senators.

[18]

http://en.wikipedia.org/wiki/Congressional_stagnation_in_the_United_States see also "Government Gridlock and Gerrymandering," John A. Lippitt, Lippitt's Policy and Politics Blog (March 9, 2014): http://lippittpolicyandpolitics.org/2014/03/09/government-gridlock-and-gerrymandering/

[19] Alan Abramowitz et al., Emory University, "Incumbency, Redistricting, and the Decline of Competition in U.S. House Elections," The Journal of Politics, Vol. 68, No. 1, Feb. 2006, pp. 75-88, p. 75.

[20] "Presidents Winning Without Popular Vote," D'Angelo Gore, FactCheck.org, (March 24, 2008): http://www.factcheck.org/2008/03/presidents-winning-without-popular-vote/

[21] http://www.redistrictingmajorityproject.com/; see also "The House the GOP Built," David Daley, New York Magazine (April 24, 2016): http://nymag.com/daily/intelligencer/2016/04/gops-house-seats-are-safe-heres-why.html

[22] "The Great Gerrymander of 2012," Sam Wang, The New York Times, SundayReview, (February 2, 2013): http://www.nytimes.com/2013/02/03/opinion/sunday/the-great-gerrymander-of-2012.html?pagewanted=all&_r=0

[23] "The Worst Voter Turnout in 72 Years," The Editorial Board, The New York Times (Nov. 11, 2014): http://mobile.nytimes.com/2014/11/12/opinion/the-worst-voter-turnout-in-72-years.html

[24] E.g., after the 2010 census, the Democrats gerrymandered in many states where they had control of the state legislature, such as in Illinois.

[25] https://en.wikipedia.org/wiki/Election_Day_(United_States)

[26] "Voting rights - The fire next time," The Economist (May 28, 2016): http://www.economist.com/news/united-states/21699451-todays-voting-rights-disputes-are-less-clear-cut-those-civil-rights-era

[27] "How Democrats Suppress The Vote - Off-year elections have much lower turnout, and Democrats prefer it that way," Eitan Hersh, fivethirtyeight.com (Nov. 3, 2015): http://fivethirtyeight.com/features/how-democrats-suppress-the-vote/

[28] "A Feasible Roadmap to Compulsory Voting," Nicholas Stephanopoulos, The Atlantic (Nov 2, 2015): http://www.theatlantic.com/politics/archive/2015/11/a-feasible-roadmap-to-compulsory-voting/413422/

[29] "Campaign Finance Reform a Tea Party Issue," Sgonsalves-brown, Public Campaign (6/20/2014): http://www.publicampaign.org/blog/2014/06/20/campaign-finance-reform-tea-party-issue; "The Tea Party is putting a conservative spin on progressive campaign finance ideas," Jon Green, America Blog (6/11/2015): http://americablog.com/2015/06/tea-party-putting-conservative-spin-progressive-campaign-finance-ideas.html

[30] "Charles Koch: This is the one issue where Bernie Sanders is right," Charles Koch, Washington Post, Opinion (2/18/2016): https://www.washingtonpost.com/opinions/charles-koch-this-is-the-one-issue-where-bernie-sanders-is-

right/2016/02/18/cdd2c228-d5c1-11e5-be55-2cc3c1e4b76b_story.html

[31] "More than Combating Corruption: The Other Benefits of Public Financing," Mimi Murray Digby Marziani, Adam Skaggs, Brennan Center for Justice, Oct. 7, 2011: https://www.brennancenter.org/analysis/more-combating-corruption-other-benefits-public-financing

[32] The Campaign Finance Center, Historical Stats; House Campaign Expenditures, 1974-2014* Nominal $, Senate Campaign Expenditures, 1974-2014* Nominal $: http://www.cfinst.org/data/historicalstats.aspx

[33] Senate incumbents have typically spent only 20-30% more, likely reflecting the higher visibility of Senate challengers, who are able to raise comparatively more than House challengers. *Id.*

[34] "For freshman in Congress, focus is on raising money," Tracy Jan, Boston Globe, May 12, 2013. https://www.bostonglobe.com/news/politics/2013/05/11/freshman-lawmakers-are-introduced-permanent-hunt-for-campaign-money/YQMMMoqCNxGKh2h0tOIF9H/story.html ; "Call Time For Congress Shows How Fundraising Dominates Bleak Work Life," Ryan Grim & Sabrina Siddiqui, Politics, Huffington Post (Jan. 8,2013): http://www.huffingtonpost.com/2013/01/08/call-time-congressional-fundraising_n_2427291.html

[35] Citizens United v. Federal Election Commission, No. 08-205, 558 U.S. 310 (2010).

[36] "Are members of Congress becoming telemarketers?" Norah O'Donnell, 60 Minutes (April 24, 2016): http://www.cbsnews.com/news/60-minutes-are-members-of-congress-becoming-telemarketers/

[37] "People hate Congress. But most incumbents get re-elected. What gives?," Chris Cillizza, The Washington Post (May 9, 2013): https://www.washingtonpost.com/news/the-fix/wp/2013/05/09/people-hate-congress-but-most-incumbents-get-re-elected-what-gives/

[38] "NRA took hard right after leadership coup,"Adam Winkler, San Francisco Chronicle (July 27, 2012):

http://m.sfgate.com/opinion/article/NRA-took-hard-right-after-leadership-coup-3741640.php

[39] See "Targeted by the NRA," CrowdPAC.com (June 10, 2015): https://www.crowdpac.com/blog/targeted-by-the-nra; see also "NRA tactics: take no prisoners," Scott Higham and Sari Horwitz, The Washington Post (May 18, 2013): http://www.washingtonpost.com/investigations/nra-tactics-take-no-prisoners/2013/05/18/4e48aad8-ace6-11e2-a198-99893f10d6dd_story.html

[40] "Strong Majority of Americans, NRA Members Back Gun Control," Seth Cline, US News and World Report (Jan. 28, 2013): http://www.usnews.com/news/articles/2013/01/28/strong-majority-of-americans-nra-members-back-gun-control

[41] "Gun production has doubled under Obama," Tim Devany, TheHill.com (July 23, 2015): http://thehill.com/regulation/248950-gun-production-has-doubled-under-obama

[42] "Labor has found a Democrat to punish on trade," Edward-Isaac Dovere, Politico (May 31, 2015): http://www.politico.com/story/2015/05/labor-targets-ami-bera-as-warning-shot-on-trade-118468

[43] "Club for Growth," Sourcewatch.com (Sept. 23, 2015): http://www.sourcewatch.org/index.php/Club_for_Growth

[44] "Teachers union helped unseat Fenty," Ben Smith, Politico (Sept. 15, 2010): http://www.politico.com/blogs/ben-smith/2010/09/teachers-union-helped-unseat-fenty-029264

[45]

http://en.wikipedia.org/wiki/History_of_lobbying_in_the_United_States

[46] "Lobbying Database," OpenSecrets.org: https://www.opensecrets.org/lobby/

[47] "Astroturf," Sourcewatch.com: http://www.sourcewatch.org/index.php/Astroturf; Read more : http://www.ehow.com/facts_5017251_definition-astroturf-lobbying.html

[48] "ANALYSIS: When a Congressman Becomes a Lobbyist, He Gets a 1,452% Raise (on Average)," Lee Fang, Republic Report (March 14, 2012). http://www.republicreport.org/2012/make-it-rain-revolving-door/ See also "ANALYSIS: When a Congressman Becomes a Lobbyist, He Gets a 1,452% Raise (on Average), ... Being a Congressman is like being an intern for lobbying." http://investmentwatchblog.com/analysis-when-a-congressman-becomes-a-lobbyist-he-gets-a-1452-raise-on-average-being-a-congressman-is-like-being-an-intern-for-lobbying/

[49] "Half of Retiring Senators Become Lobbyists, Up 1,500% in 40 Years," Mike Flynn, Breitbart.com (July 29, 2013): http://www.breitbart.com/big-government/2013/07/29/half-of-retiring-senators-become-lobbyists-up-1500-in-40-years/

[50] See "Campaign Contributions vs. Lobbying Expenses," Timothy Taylor, Conversable Economist (Sept. 4, 2012): http://conversableeconomist.blogspot.com/2012/09/campaign-contributions-vs-lobbying.html; see also "Wall Street's Campaign Contributions and Lobbyist Expenditures," Center for Responsive Politics, SourceWatch.com: http://wallstreetwatch.org/reports/part2.pdf

[51] "Why Congress Relies on Lobbyists Instead of Thinking for Itself," Lee Drutman and Steven Teles, The Atlantic (March 10, 2015): http://www.theatlantic.com/politics/archive/2015/03/when-congress-cant-think-for-itself-it-turns-to-lobbyists/387295/

[52] *Id.*

[53] *Id.*

[54] Republican senator Tom Coburn estimated that every $1 spent on the GAO (General Accounting Office) produces $90 in savings recommendations. *Id.*

[55] Article One, Section 5 of the Constitution simply says "Each House may determine the rules of its proceedings..." and that a majority of the Senate constitutes a quorum to do business.

[56] https://en.wikipedia.org/wiki/Filibuster_in_the_United_States_Senate

[57] "Cloture" was adopted as a rule to allow ending a filibuster. It originally required 2/3 of the Senate, which was almost never attained. The Senate tried eleven times between 1927 and 1962 to invoke cloture but failed each time. https://en.wikipedia.org/wiki/Cloture#United_States . In 1975, the Democratic Senate majority changed the rule on cloture to reduce the majority required to the current 60 (which has been attained, but rarely).

[58] http://en.wikipedia.org/wiki/Filibuster_%28United_States%29#Recent_U.S._Senate_history

[59] "Senate May End an Era of Cloakroom Anonymity," Carl Hulse, The New York Times (Aug. 2, 2007): http://www.nytimes.com/2007/08/02/washington/02ethics.html?_r=0

[60] https://en.wikipedia.org/wiki/Senate_hold

[61] "Sloan: Secret Holds Are Filibuster's Silent Partner in Stalling, Melanie Sloan, Rollcall.com (Jan. 23, 2013): http://www.rollcall.com/news/sloan_secret_holds_are_filibusters_silent_partner_in_stalling-221053-1.html

[62] "Senate passes budget bill repealing Obamacare, defunding Planned Parenthood," Ted Barrett, Fox13 (Dec. 3, 2015): http://fox13now.com/2015/12/03/senate-passes-budget-bill-repealing-obamacare-defunding-planned-parenthood/

[63] "Keystone XL Backfires On Republicans As Democrats Move To Turn Pipeline Into A Real Jobs Bill," Jason Easley, Politicususa.com (Jan. 5, 2015): http://www.politicususa.com/2015/01/05/keystone-xl-backfires-republicans-democrats-move-turn-pipeline-real-jobs-bill.html

[64] "The Congressional Earmark Ban: the Real Bridge to Nowhere | Commentary," Steven C. LaTourette, Roll Call (July 30, 2014): http://www.rollcall.com/news/the_congressional_earmark_ban_the_real_bridge_to_nowhere_commentary-235380-1.html

[65] https://en.wikipedia.org/wiki/Lincoln_(2012_film)

[66] "How American Politics Went Insane," Jonathan Rauch, The Atlantic (July/August 2016): http://www.theatlantic.com/magazine/archive/2016/07/how-american-politics-went-insane/485570/ .

[67] "The Congressional Earmark Ban: the Real Bridge to Nowhere | Commentary," Steven C. LaTourette, Roll Call (July 30, 2014): http://www.rollcall.com/news/the_congressional_earmark_ban_t he_real_bridge_to_nowhere_commentary-235380-1.html

[68] "The idea that Washington would work better if there were TV cameras monitoring every conversation gets it exactly wrong," Tom Daschle quote in "How American Politics Went Insane," Jonathan Rauch, The Atlantic (July/August 2016): http://www.theatlantic.com/magazine/archive/2016/07/how-american-politics-went-insane/485570/

[69] "4 Simple Steps to End Political Gridlock," Jason Grumet, U.S. News & World Report (Oct. 29, 2014): http://www.usnews.com/opinion/articles/2014/10/29/end-washington-gridlock-with-compromise-and-earmarks

[70] "A simple way to fix gridlock in Congress -- change committees," Brian Feinstein, LA Times (Jan. 4, 2015): http://www.latimes.com/opinion/op-ed/la-oe-feinstein-congress-committees-random-assignment-20150105-story.html

[71] Article I, section 9, clause 7 states that "No money shall be drawn from the Treasury, but in Consequence of Appropriations made by Law; and a regular Statement and Account of Receipts and ," Expenditures of all public Money shall be published from time to time."

[72] See: "The Long Story of U.S. Debt, From 1790 to 2011, in 1 Little Chart," Matt Phillips, The Atlantic, Nov. 13, 2012): http://www.theatlantic.com/business/archive/2012/11/the-long-story-of-us-debt-from-1790-to-2011-in-1-little-chart/265185/

[73] The government actually uses a "modified cash basis": "Why we need accrual accounting in Washington," former Rep. Joseph J. DioGuardi (R-N.Y.), Thehill.com (Sept. 13, 2013): http://thehill.com/blogs/congress-blog/economy-a-budget/322139-why-we-need-accrual-accounting-in-washington

[74] "Social Security's trust funds are expected to be depleted in 2034, unchanged from the trustees' projection a year ago. Medicare's trust fund for inpatient care will be exhausted in 2028, two years earlier than previously projected." "Trustees: Tiny rise in Social Security benefits next year," Ricardo Alonso-Zaldivar and Stephen Ohlemacher, Yahoo! Finance (June 22, 2016): http://finance.yahoo.com/news/trustees-meager-hike-social-security-benefits-next-143202462--finance.html

[75] https://www.ssa.gov/oact/trsum/

[76] These numbers will have changed by the time of publishing of this book. See http://www.justfacts.com/nationaldebt.asp

[77] "That happened in 1999, when legislation proposing a retroactive pension increase for state employees was introduced in the California Legislature. Accrual accounting would've forced state officials to acknowledge a large expense in the 1999 budget as a result of the legislation. But because the state employed cash accounting and no cash changed hands that year, the deal was hidden from that year's budget. The legislation was quietly enacted into law without notice that elected officials had just transferred tens of billions of dollars to a special interest." "What Accrual Accounting Would've Exposed," David Crane, Fox & Hounds (Feb. 26, 2016): http://www.foxandhoundsdaily.com/2016/02/what-accrual-accounting-wouldve-exposed/ See also: http://www.hjta.org/news/opinion-what-accrual-accounting-wouldve-exposed/

[78] "Why we need accrual accounting in Washington," By former Rep. Joseph J. DioGuardi, The Hill (9/13/2013): http://thehill.com/blogs/congress-blog/economy-a-budget/322139-why-we-need-accrual-accounting-in-washington

[79] https://en.wikipedia.org/wiki/Earmark_(politics) This site allows browsing or searching for particular earmarks: "Earmarks," Office of Management and Budget: https://earmarks.omb.gov/earmarks-public/

[80] See, e.g., "Flawed F-35 Too Big to Kill as Lockheed Hooks 45 States," Kathleen Miller, Tony Capaccio and Danielle Ivory, Bloomberg.com (Feb. 22, 2013):

http://www.bloomberg.com/news/2013-02-22/flawed-f-35-fighter-too-big-to-kill-as-lockheed-hooks-45-states.html ; see also "This Map Shows Why The F-35 Has Turned Into A Trillion-Dollar Fiasco," Jeremy Bender, Armin Rosen and Skye Gould, Businessinsider.com (Aug. 20, 2014): http://www.businessinsider.com/this-map-explains-the-f-35-fiasco-2014-8; see also https://en.wikipedia.org/wiki/Lockheed_Martin_F-35_Lightning_II

[81] "As Companies Seek Tax Deals, Governments Pay High Price," Louise Story, The New York Times (Dec. 1, 2012): http://www.nytimes.com/2012/12/02/us/how-local-taxpayers-bankroll-corporations.html?pagewanted=all&_r=1

[82] There would be a benefit for the states collectively in the rare instance where the jobs would go overseas, instead of another state. See "Tax Incentives: Costly for States, Drag on the Nation," Institute on Taxation and Economic Policy, itep.org (Aug. 14, 2013): http://itep.org/itep_reports/archives.html

[83] The odd thing is that the Court ruled that the law which allowed Marbury to bring his case to the Supreme Court was unconstitutional because Congress, in passing the law, tried to expand the jurisdiction the Court was given under the Constitution (while the Court itself expanded its jurisdiction in denying Congress the ability to expand its jurisdiction). The case involved Marbury being appointed justice of the peace by president John Adams, but the appointment wasn't delivered before the end of Adam's term. The suit tried to force the new Secretary of State, James Madison, to deliver the appointment. The Court held that the act of Congress enabling Marbury to bring his claim to the Supreme Court was itself unconstitutional, since it extended the Supreme Court's jurisdiction beyond what was set forth in the Constitution. See https://en.wikipedia.org/wiki/Marbury_v._Madison

[84] In the early 1800's, the big issues were power struggles between the states and the federal government. The court issued a number of decisions that confirmed the supremacy of the Federal government, such as striking down state attempts to tax the

131

national bank and saying federal law was controlling for interstate commerce (river steamboat permits). The courts have found that various administrative actions require due process under the Constitution (14th amendment, adopted in 1868), and have steadily expanded the types of actions that require due process. During the New Deal, the Court blocked a number of Franklin Roosevelt's attempts to bring the country out of the Great Depression, leading to Roosevelt's failed attempt to pack the Supreme Court by adding more justices who would be friendly (the number of judges isn't set in the Constitution). In 1954, the Court struck down segregation laws, something Congress had considered since the Civil War, but failed to do (blocked by the minority population in the south through their filibustering in the Senate). In 1974, the Supreme Court ruled that the President is subject to the judicial process, rejecting President Nixon's claim of immunity and forcing him to hand over the tapes which led to his impeachment. This legislation by the courts is something no other liberal democracy does[84], likely due to the fact that they have a single body parliament that then elects a president or prime minister, and thus they are actually able to get something done.

[85] 55 year lifespan for 5 year olds was the number in 1845, the earliest the data is available: See "Life Expectancy," Our World in Data, ourworldindata.org:
http://ourworldindata.org/data/population-growth-vital-statistics/life-expectancy/

[86] The "advice and consent" language came from the use of "executive councils," but instead, this power was given to the Senate by the "Committee on Remaining Matters" of the Constitutional Convention during its last days, to avoid creating a new body (executive council). See ""Advice & Consent"? No One Really Knows What the Founders Had in Mind," Ray Raphael, History News Network (2/21/2016):
http://historynewsnetwork.org/article/162068

[87] "Split Supreme Court blocks Obama immigration plan," Lawrence Hurley, Reuters (June 24, 2016):
http://mobile.reuters.com/article/idUSKCN0Z91P4

[88] The Public Works Committee also was given control over particular contracts. Attempts to reorganize the government to improve efficiency by Presidents Hoover and Roosevelt and subsequent presidents were granted, but subject to Congressional approval of particular actions. By the time of the Carter Administration, in response to public complaints about excessive government regulations, Congress was threatening to extend the legislative veto to cover every regulation by federal agencies. President Carter chose to support a challenge to one of those, a legislative veto by just one house of Congress over an administrative decision to suspend the deportation of Chadha, a student who overstayed his student visa. Congress had granted the INS this authority, but the law permitted either house of Congress to disapprove of any particular Attorney General decision. See *supra*.

[89] "Legislative Vetoes After Chadha." Louis Fisher, Senior Specialist in Separation of Powers Government and Finance Division, CRS Report for Congress (May 2, 2005): http://www.loufisher.org/docs/lv/4116.pdf

[90] Francis Fukuyama, "Political Order and Political Decay," p. 475 (2014)

[91] Fukuyama, "Political Order and Political Decay," p. 476 (2014)

[92] https://en.wikipedia.org/wiki/Base_Realignment_and_Closure

[93] Many people think the most obvious example of the President usurping the power of Congress is undeclared wars, since the power to declare war is expressly given to Congress in the Constitution. However, these were usually authorized by Congress (Vietnam war, 1st & 2nd Iraq wars, Afghanistan war, etc.). After the Vietnam war, the War Powers Act of 1973 passed Congress, limiting the number of troops the President could commit without authorization, and it has been generally adhered to. But there are other encroachments on the Congress' role.

[94] The President has "executive power" (U.S. Constitution, Article II, Section 1, Clause 1) and is required to "take Care that the Laws be faithfully executed" (Article II, Section 3, Clause 5). He/she is also the "Commander in Chief" (Article II, Section 2).

[95] Congress was not in session, and Washington did not want to wait. Congress later concurred with the Neutrality Act of 1794

[96] The Emancipation Proclamation freed the slaves in the South, with Lincoln claiming his constitutional powers as Commander in Chief in time of war. Lincoln is said to have a chink in his halo for issuing a proclamation suspending habeas corpus (allowing the government to detain people indefinitely without a trial). Certain legislators and others sympathetic to the Confederacy were targeted, because they were trying to keep union troops from moving through Maryland to defend Washington D.C. which sits between the borders of Maryland and Virginia, and Lincoln was worried about an imminent invasion from Virginia. The Supreme Court ruled that the President didn't have that authority, only Congress did. Lincoln ignored the Court and Congress later passed a suspension.

[97] Teddy Roosevelt also used executive orders to suspend or amend the civil service rules to exempt certain agencies (e.g., the Navy) or particular individuals.

[98] Franklin Roosevelt issued executive orders during the New Deal, establishing various agencies and regulating the economy (e.g., the Works Progress Administration, enacted by E.O. 7034 in 1935). Most were with Congressional cooperation. For example, on his first day in office, Roosevelt issued a proclamation closing all banks for four days to give time to implement his New deal financial restructuring.

[99] The lower court issued a preliminary injunction, which allowed the early appeal without waiting for a trial. Justice Jackson's concurring opinion in the Youngstown case has been the most influential. He described 3 categories of executive orders:

    1. Orders based on express or implied authorization from Congress have maximum presumption of validity. The courts have given the President great leeway in the areas of foreign policy and national security.

    2. "Twilight Zone" actions, absent Congressional grant, based in inherent powers – the presumption is fact-dependent. It

is strong if based on powers recited in the Constitution as Commander in Chief, for example.

3. Orders contrary to express or implied will of Congress are unlikely to be valid.

[100] Truman issued Executive Order 9981 to desegregate the military. The order was justified under his power as Commander in Chief to determine the best way to assign soldiers to units.

[101] "The Stunning Triumph of Cost-Benefit Analysis," Cass Sunstein, Bloomberg View (Sept. 12, 2012): http://www.bloombergview.com/articles/2012-09-12/the-stunning-triumph-of-cost-benefit-analysis

[102] The military commission executive order was held to violate the Uniform Code of Military Justice and the Geneva Convention. This was in spite of Congressional support, including the Detainee Treatment Act of 2005 which tried to prevent the Supreme Court from hearing any cases brought by Guantanamo prisoners.

[103] "Playing presidential Ping-Pong with executive orders," Phillip J. Cooper, Washington Post, Opinions (Jan. 31, 2014): https://www.washingtonpost.com/opinions/playing-presidential-ping-pong-with-executive-orders/2014/01/31/cbb6fe30-89f3-11e3-a5bd-844629433ba3_story.html

[104] Another example was a bill exempting religious groups with federal grants from discrimination rules that were against their precepts. It failed in the Senate, but Bush enacted it with executive order 13279. Some executive orders are secret, and not published, for national security purposes. It was later revealed that Bush had issued an executive order in 2002 (after the 9-11-2001 World Trade Center terrorist attack) allowing the NSA to tap the phones of terrorist suspects, including US citizens, without a warrant.

[105] He expanded the ages and arrival dates of those eligible in a Nov. 2014 executive order, shielding an additional 5 million illegal immigrants from deportation.

[106] Other examples are the use of a memorandum to declare Bristol Bay, Alaska, off-limits to oil and gas exploration, raising

the minimum wage for federal contractors, and prohibiting discrimination against gays by the federal government and federal contractors.

[107] Larry M. Bartels, "Unequal Democracy, The Political Economy of the New Gilded Age," p. 220. (2010)

[108] ABA Task Force on Presidential Signing Statements, Recommendation, p. 8 (2006)

[109] https://en.m.wikipedia.org/wiki/Signing_statement

[110] American Bar Association Report, Adopted by the House of Delegates, Aug. 7-8, 2006: http://www.americanbar.org/content/dam/aba/migrated/leadership/2006/annual/dailyjournal/20060823144113.authcheckdam.pdf ; see also https://en.wikipedia.org/wiki/Signing_statement

[111] Erik Black, Imperfect Union, Kindle edition, location 2048.

[112] "Outrageous bills - Why Congress writes such long laws," The Economist, Nov 23rd 2013: http://www.economist.com/news/united-states/21590368-why-congress-writes-such-long-laws-outrageous-bills

[113] One of the reasons may be an unintended consequence of the 2010 Congressional moratorium on earmarks. Without the ability to use those to buy votes, fewer bills pass, and those that do have over 500 members of Congress trying to add an amendment favorable to their position on some issue. For example, the 2009 Senate immigration bill contained sections on global health-care co-operation, on the protection of family values in programs to apprehend illegal migrants, and the treatment of Filipino veterans of the second world war. Id. It is not only a (1) complex process to enact laws and (2) complexity in the laws themselves. The implementing regulations (3) are also long and complex. The Dodd-Frank regulations were already over 22,000 pages by 2015 ("5 Numbers To Know As Dodd-Frank Wall Street Reform Celebrates Its 5th Birthday." Alan Pyke, Think Progress, July 21, 2015: http://thinkprogress.org/economy/2015/07/21/3682696/dodd-frank-five-years-2/), with more mandated regulations to be written (see "Three Years In, Dodd-Frank Deadlines Missed As Page Count Rises," Joe Mont, Compliance Week (July 22, 2013):

https://www.complianceweek.com/blogs/the-filing-cabinet/three-years-in-dodd-frank-deadlines-missed-as-page-count-rises). Those pages of regulations impose on companies a 4th layer of complexity, even more pages of required compliance. For example, a 298-page proposed regulation for the 11 pages of the law specifying the "Volcker rule" (reducing banks' ability to take excessive risks) includes 383 explicit questions for firms which break down into 1,420 sub-questions ("The Dodd-Frank act - Too big not to fail," The Economist (Feb. 18, 2012): http://www.economist.com/node/21547784).

[114] They want to point to laws they passed to deal with all the issues their constituents complain about. The best solution is often just better enforcement of existing laws, or ignoring what are often outlier exceptions, but these don't build a resume and talking points for re-election. Another factor causing complexity is the admirable quest for justice in the U.S., and a desire for the rule of law where you can look up the correct answer to everything and address every unfairness, no matter how small. But each unforeseen circumstance and exception handled with a new law or regulation creates a new unforeseen circumstance that needs to be dealt with.

[115] On top of the above, special interest lobbying for a wide variety of exceptions adds to the complexity, making compliance much more difficult for everyone so they can get their goodies (the tax code being Exhibit A). There is a Catch-22, or feedback loop, with each loophole being addressed with a new, complex law with new loopholes. This gives special interests even more opportunities in the ever increasing levels of complexity.

[116] The rich are also the only ones with both the resources and enough at stake to make it worthwhile to invest in lobbying, which increases their advantage. As a result, the US ranks last in access to justice among both its income group (richest 11 countries) and region (North America and Europe).The US is last in the high income group and region (North America and Western Europe) in The Rule of Law Index (World Justice Project) with respect to access to justice – "U.S. Lags Behind Other Wealthy Nations in Rule of Law Index," By James

Podgers, ABA Journal (Dec 1, 2010). See:
http://www.abajournal.com/mobile/mag_article/playing_catch-up_us_lags_other_nations_in_rule_of_law_index
While the effort to address every unfairness is admirable for preventing some individual injustices, it has the cumulative effect of strangling small businesses and the economy. Everyone has to comply with the complexity that exists for the one in a million exception.
A study in Los Angeles, for example, showed that it can take months or years to jump over all the regulatory hurdles to open a restaurant. There are business licenses, zoning requirements, scores of permits and approvals and a seemingly endless number of taxes and fees. At least a dozen government agencies must be dealt with. The process is so complex, the city published a 147-page handbook to explain it. See "Politico: Regulations Stifle Economic Growth," John Allison, Politico (Oct. 5, 2011): http://www.ronjohnson.senate.gov/public/index.cfm/2011/10/regulations-stifle-economic-growth

[117] "Out of Control Federal Regulations Stifle Economy," Gary D. Halbert, FORECASTS & TRENDS E-LETTER (Sept. 16, 2014): http://forecastsandtrends.com/printarticle.php/922/

[118] "Ten Facts You Should Know About the Federal Estate Tax," Chye-Ching Huang and Brandon DeBot, Center on Budget and Policy Priorities (March 23, 2015): http://www.cbpp.org/cms/?fa=view&id=2655

[119] Al Gore, The Assault on Reason, p. 79 (2007). See also "A Guide to the Bush Administration's Environmental Doublespeak" (Oct. 2004): http://www.southshore.com/baedd.htm

[120] "A Guide to the Bush Administration's Environmental Doublespeak" (Oct. 2004): http://www.southshore.com/baedd.htm

[121] http://ballotpedia.org/Arizona_Non-Smoker_Protection,_Proposition_206_(2006)

[122] National Institute on Money in State Politics, CALIFORNIANS FOR AFFORDABLE PRESCRIPTIONS YES ON PROPOSITION 78: http://host-69-144-32-180.kls-mt.client.bresnan.net/database/uniquecommittee.phtml?uct=633&so9=y

[123] When local governments worried about the obesity epidemic started considering taxes on sugary drinks, did Coke lobby with the message that this would hurt its profits? No, they sponsored ads emphasizing exercise over diet, and funded an "independent" nutrition organization, Global Energy Balance Network, which published opinions that sugary drinks are not the cause of obesity. See "Nutrition Expert Attacks Coca-Cola's Research Funding," Darlene Tverdohleb, The Science Times (Aug 10, 2015): http://www.sciencetimes.com/articles/7051/20150810/nutrition-expert-coca-colas-research-funding.htm

[124] Centers for Medicare & Medicaid Services, National Health Expenditure Data, Historical: https://www.cms.gov/research-statistics-data-and-systems/statistics-trends-and-reports/nationalhealthexpenddata/nationalhealthaccountshistorical.html

[125] "Clinton health care plan of 1993," Wikipedia: https://en.m.wikipedia.org/wiki/Clinton_health_care_plan_of_1993

[126] "Under The Influence," Steve Kroft, 60 Minutes, CBS News (March 29, 2007): http://www.cbsnews.com/news/under-the-influence/

[127] "The unstoppable rise in lobbying by American business is bad for business itself," Schumpeter, The Exonomist (June 13, 2015): http://www.economist.com/news/business/21654067-unstoppable-rise-lobbying-american-business-bad-business-itself-washington

[128] https://en.wikipedia.org/wiki/Medicare_Part_D

[129] "The Cost of Cancer Drugs," Lesley Stahl, 60 Minutes (June 21, 2015): http://www.cbsnews.com/news/cost-of-cancer-drugs-60-minutes-lesley-stahl-health-care/

[130] *Id.*

[131] "A hard-hitting anti-Obamacare ad makes a claim that doesn't add up, Glenn Kessler, The Washington Post (Feb. 20, 2014): http://www.washingtonpost.com/blogs/fact-checker/wp/2014/02/20/a-hard-hitting-anti-obamacare-ad-makes-a-claim-that-doesnt-add-up/

[132] "The Top 10 lobbying victories of 2010," Kevin Bogardus, The Hill (Dec. 15, 2010): http://thehill.com/business-a-lobbying/133691-the-top-10-lobbying-victories-of-2010

[133] *Id.*, http://thehill.com/business-a-lobbying/133691-the-top-10-lobbying-victories-of-2010

[134] "America's Bitter Pill," by Steven Brill. See "'America's Bitter Pill,' by Steven Brill," Zephyr Teachout, The New York Times, Sunday Book Review (Jan. 7, 2015): http://www.nytimes.com/2015/01/11/books/review/americas-bitter-pill-by-steven-brill.html?_r=1

[135] "The Sabotage Device Within Obamacare," Ed Kilgore, Washington Monthly (March 5, 2013): http://www.washingtonmonthly.com/political-animal-a/2013_03/the_sabotage_device_within_oba043367.php

[136] Sourcewatch.com "Cato Institute": http://www.sourcewatch.org/index.php/Cato_Institute

[137] Cato Institute, Policy Analysis: http://www.cato.org/pubs/pas/html/pa638/pa63800013.html

[138] Sourcewatch.com "American Enterprise Institute": http://www.sourcewatch.org/index.php/American_Enterprise_Institute

[139] "The FDA Should Not Mandate Comparative-Effectiveness Trials," Scott Gottlieb, American Enterprise Institute (June 15, 2011): https://www.aei.org/publication/the-fda-should-not-mandate-comparative-effectiveness-trials/

140

http://ballotpedia.org/California_Proposition_98,_Mandatory_Ed ucation_Spending_(1988)
[141] "Cost to fire a tenured teacher? More than $219,000,"Scott Reeder, The Hidden Costs of Tenure (2005): http://thehiddencostsoftenure.com/stories/?prcss=display&id=295 712

[142] "Can Vergara fix our schools?", Lisa Davis, California Lawyer (Aug. 2015): http://www.callawyer.com/2015/08/can-vergara-v-california-fix-our-schools/ .
[143] "What has changed, and what has not," Caroline M. Hoxby, Our Schools, & Our Future, pp. 74, 99 (2003).
[144] "The Downfall of For-Profit Colleges," Alia Wong, The Atlantic (Feb. 23, 2015): http://www.theatlantic.com/education/archive/2015/02/the-downfall-of-for-profit-colleges/385810/

[145] "Credit Supply and the Rise in College Tuition: Evidence from the Expansion in Federal Student Aid Programs," David O. Lucca, Taylor Nadauld, and Karen Shen, Federal Reserve Bank of New York (newyorkfed.com) (July 2015, No. 733, revised March 2016): http://www.newyorkfed.org/research/staff_reports/sr733.html

[146] "End the Mortgage Interest Deduction? Expect a Fight," Mark Koba, CNBC, Thursday, 28 Feb 2013, http://www.cnbc.com/id/100506426
[147] "Kill the mortgage deduction and give it to entrepreneurs," John Wasik, Reuters Money (Feb. 11, 2011): http://blogs.reuters.com/reuters-wealth/2011/02/11/kill-the-mortgage-deduction-and-give-it-to-entrepreneurs/
[148] "Steve Coll: How Exxon Shaped the Climate Debate," Jason M. Breslow, Frontline (Oct. 23, 2012): http://www.pbs.org/wgbh/pages/frontline/environment/climate-of-doubt/steve-coll-how-exxon-shaped-the-climate-debate/

[149] "What Exxon knew about the Earth's melting Arctic," Sara Jerving, Katie Jennings, Masako Melissa Hirsch and Susanne Rust, Los Angeles Times (Oct. 9, 2015): http://graphics.latimes.com/exxon-arctic/
[150] ""Dark Money" Funds Climate Change Denial Effort," Douglas Fischer, Scientific American (Dec. 23, 2013): http://www.scientificamerican.com/article/dark-money-funds-climate-change-denial-effort/
[151] "The Price of Prison Guard Unions," Amanda Carey, Capital Research Center, Labor Watch (October 2011) http://capitalresearch.org/2011/10/the-price-of-prison-guard-unions-2/
[152] "A Primer: Three Strikes - The Impact After More Than a Decade," Legislative Analyst's Office, California's Nonpartisan Fiscal and Policy Advisor, October 2005: http://www.lao.ca.gov/2005/3_strikes/3_strikes_102005.htm "The overall crime rate in California, as measured by the Department of Justice's California Crime Index, began declining before the passage of the Three Strikes law. In fact, the overall crime rate declined by 10 percent between 1991 and 1994. The crime rate continued to decline after Three Strikes, ..."
[153] "Policy Basics: Where Do Our Federal Tax Dollars Go?" Center on Budget and Policy Priorities (updated March 11, 2015): http://www.cbpp.org/research/policy-basics-where-do-our-federal-tax-dollars-go?fa=view&id=1258
[154] "Politics and Defense Capabilities," Maj. Brian R. Davis, USMC, Strategic Studies Quarterly, Fall 2014: http://www.au.af.mil/au/ssq/digital/pdf/fall_2014/Davis.pdf
[155] "Politics and Defense Capabilities," Maj. Brian R. Davis, USMC, Strategic Studies Quarterly, Fall 2014, pp. 102-107: http://www.au.af.mil/au/ssq/digital/pdf/fall_2014/Davis.pdf
[155] "Cost to fire a tenured teacher? More than $219,000," Scott Reeder, The Hidden Costs of Tenure, An investigative report by Small Newspaper Group (2005): http://thehiddencostsoftenure.com/stories/?prcss=display&id=295712

[156] See, e.g., "Investments Can Yield More on K Street, Study Indicates," Dan Eggen, Washington Post (April 12, 2009): http://www.washingtonpost.com/wp-dyn/content/article/2009/04/11/AR2009041102035.html

[157] "Charles Koch: This is the one issue where Bernie Sanders is right," Charles Koch, Washington Post, Opinion (2/18/2016): https://www.washingtonpost.com/opinions/charles-koch-this-is-the-one-issue-where-bernie-sanders-is-right/2016/02/18/cdd2c228-d5c1-11e5-be55-2cc3c1e4b76b_story.html

[158] Bartels, Unequal Democracy, electronic p. 163.

[159] It has been argued that tax cuts pay for themselves by stimulating investment and thus the tax revenue from those investments, even at a lower tax rate, would be higher. But that hasn't happened. A lower tax rate is provided on capital gains and interest, with the claimed economic stimulus benefits debunked. There was a temporary increase in capital gains tax revenue right after the 2003 tax cuts. But that was just people with one-time sales of stocks to take advantage of the new low rates, fearful that higher rates might return. In the long term, there was a loss of revenue ($50 billion lost over 10 years for 5% cut in rate). See "Evidence Shows That Tax Cuts Lose Revenue," Center on Budget and Policy Priorities (revised July 21, 2008): http://www.cbpp.org/research/evidence-shows-that-tax-cuts-lose-revenue; A coincidental bull market increased revenue with increasing stock prices, similar to Europe, which had no capital gains tax cut). See also "Would a Capital Gains Tax Cut Stimulate The Economy?" Joel Friedman, Iris Lav, and Peter Orszag, Center on Budget and Policy Priorities (Sept. 20, 2001) http://www.cbpp.org/archives/9-20-01tax.htm

[160] "Q.What is carried interest, and should it be taxed as capital gain?" Tax Policy Center, Urban Institute & Brookings Institution, Briefing Book: http://www.taxpolicycenter.org/briefing-book/what-carried-interest-and-how-should-it-be-taxed

[161] If you think about it and apply a little common sense, there are basically two types of investments. One is venture capital and

companies buying machinery and other capital goods to expand, which does lift the economy. The other is simply the buying and selling of stocks and real estate. Other than venture capital and the Initial Public Offering (IPO) where the company is raising money, none of that money for stock sales goes to the company to invest in machinery, people, etc. It is simply money changing hands between investors. The vast majority of capital gains relate to the sale of real estate and stock in well-established companies, not venture capital. That doesn't stimulate anything other than the stock market prices and real estate prices. The result? 95% of the benefit of lower capital gains and dividends taxes goes to those making over $200,000 per year (see Appendix I).

[162] "The Misguided Crusade to Kill the Estate Tax," Chad Stone, US News & World Report (March 27, 2015): http://www.usnews.com/opinion/economic-intelligence/2015/03/27/facts-dont-back-estate-tax-repeal ; see also "Pro-McConnell group says the estate tax makes it hard for family farms to survive," Steve Contorno, Politifact (April 3, 2014): http://www.politifact.com/truth-o-meter/statements/2014/apr/03/kentucky-opportunity-coalition/pro-mcconnell-group-says-estate-tax-makes-it-hard-/

[163] "These 6 Corporations Control 90% Of The Media In America," Ashley Lutz, Business Insider, June 14, 2012: http://www.businessinsider.com/these-6-corporations-control-90-of-the-media-in-america-2012-6

[164] See "The Withering Watchdog," Laura Frank, PBS (June, 2009): http://www.pbs.org/wnet/expose/2009/06/the-withering-watchdog.html

[165] Some have argued that the media has a conflict of interest. Media outlets receive a lot of revenue for political ads, and may not be inclined to launch investigative reporting against their sponsors. In 2012, CBS's profits rose by $180 million due to the boom in political advertising after Citizens United. "The New Price of American Politics," James Bennet, p. 80, The Atlantic (Oct. 2012): http://www.theatlantic.com/magazine/archive/2012/10/the/309086/

[166] I borrowed this expression from Bill Clinton's internal campaign motto during his successful run for president. See: https://en.m.wikipedia.org/wiki/It%27s_the_economy,_stupid
[167] Government also builds the infrastructure needed for capitalism – the roads, railroads, bridges, ports, etc. (with special interests both taking advantage of the free infrastructure, and getting the contracts to build them). The government provides a judicial system to enforce contracts and property rights upon which capitalism is based. Government also provides a financial system backed by the Federal Reserve; deposit insurance; patents and other intellectual property rights, etc. The government today also pays for many costs that enable businesses to be successful: public schools to train workers; university research to enable new technologies; limited liability for corporations; bankruptcy protection – the list goes on and on. Before public schools, companies would train their own employees. Before corporate limited liability laws, business lenders could come after the personal assets of the investors, discouraging entrepreneurs. All of us pay for this with our taxes, and thus we provide the advantages to those that succeed under Capitalism. At the same time, special interests have rigged the tax system so they don't pay as much, thus reaping the double benefit of (1) getting special advantages provided by influencing government, (2) without having to pay for it.
[168] The recent book "Capital" by economist Thomas Pickery provides data that shows that capital has historically grown more than wages. He studied income and wealth data over hundreds of years. He says that the return on capital has exceeded economic growth (and thus wages) throughout that time (except for the period of the economic shocks of World Wars I & II and the Great Depression, which temporarily reduced the value of capital). Capital growing faster than wages would show up in an increasing gap between rich and poor, which is what we are seeing. But we don't need Pickery's book to show this – we just need to use our common sense. Companies by design try to increase profits (return on capital), and drive down costs, which means hold down wages and numbers of employees. Thus the

inherent mechanism is to favor capital at the expense of wages. Competition can lessen this effect, but not if stymied through undue influence of the government.
[169] "For most workers, real wages have barely budged for decades,"Drew DeSilver, Fact Tank (Oct. 9, 2014): http://www.pewresearch.org/fact-tank/2014/10/09/for-most-workers-real-wages-have-barely-budged-for-decades/
[170] Without government intervention, there has always been excessive concentration of wealth – an unregulated nuclear reaction. The concentration of wealth is not unique to capitalism, or to the present. Over human history, the most natural state has been a few rich rulers and their cohorts, and a lot of poor peasants or slaves. The natural economic state has been to have someone seize most of the assets and impoverish the rest of us, whether it be a king, a dictator or the mafia. Even with many supposed democracies today, many are rigged so that the president is in fact a dictator, manipulating the public through state controlled media, with privileges going to his/her buddies.

In Russia, "president" Putin is running a corrupt kleptocracy, with all his buddies, the Russian oligarchs, getting most of the economic benefits. The state controlled media and censorship of other sources actually keeps him popular among ordinary Russians. "President" Hugo Chavez in Venezuela ran the country's economy into the ground, destroying the middle class with unsustainable giveaways to the majority poor, which kept him in power (along with, of course, state controlled media). France is often held hostage by the transportation and other public unions. India is a democracy, but is the most over-regulated country in the world.

In the U.S., the rigging is more subtle, but it is there. If the US special interest control continues to grow, we risk ending up like these other countries. The birth of the US embarked us on a novel experiment in Democracy, and bucked the trend of dictators and kings. But things have been returning to the more natural state of insider influence, because special interests have been gaming the system and we haven't adjusted. In the U.S., we don't have problems to the degree of other countries – yet. The influence is more subtle, but very effective. Instead of Russian oligarchs we have special interests that amass great wealth through government lobbying. We have public unions that aren't as powerful as in France, but have gotten unsustainable pensions (this is one of the reasons Detroit went bankrupt). We don't have state-controlled media, but we've had a huge consolidation of the media (a few large companies have bought up all the formerly independent newspapers, TV and radio stations) and we have huge media influence (e.g., buying ads) by special interests. We don't have over-regulation to the extent of India, but we're catching up fast. As a result of all these problems, we are losing our competitive advantage over other countries.

[171] "The Winner-Take-All Society: Why the Few at the Top Get So Much More Than the Rest of Us," Robert Frank and Philip Cook (Penguin Books, 1996)
[172] "The Bully Pulpit," Doris Kearns Goodwin, p. 191.
[173]

http://www.regentsprep.org/regents/ushisgov/themes/reform/progressive.htm
[174] Claims that the minimum wage adversely affects job growth have been shown to be wrong: Unequal Democracy, Larry M. Bartels, 2008, Kindle location 4925 .
[175] "Why Did Henry Ford Double His Minimum Wage?" Jeff Nilsson, The Saturday Evening Post (January 3, 2014): http://www.saturdayeveningpost.com/2014/01/03/history/post-perspective/ford-doubles-minimum-wage.html
[176] "Richer and Poorer, the Accounting for inequality," Jill Lepore, The New Yorker, March 16, 2015: http://www.newyorker.com/magazine/2015/03/16/richer-and-poorer
[177] "Fed: Gap Between Rich, Poor Americans Widened During Recovery," Ben Leubsdorf, The Wall Street Journal, Sept. 4, 2014: http://www.wsj.com/articles/fed-gap-between-rich-poor-americans-widened-during-recovery-1409853628. Note the disparity in date ranges is due to my inability to find the multiple

measures in one article, not any intent to manipulate you. But good for you if you noticed this!

[178] "US and Israel have worst inequality in the developed world," Alanna Petroff, CNN Money, May 21, 2015: http://money.cnn.com/2015/05/21/news/economy/worst-inequality-countries-oecd/

[179] The rich and the rest - American inequality is a tale of two countries, The Economist (Oct. 13, 2012): http://www.economist.com/node/21564418

[180] "Graph: How the Financial Sector Consumed America's Economic Growth," Benjamin Landy, The Century Foundation (Feb. 25, 2013: https://tcf.org/content/commentary/graph-how-the-financial-sector-consumed-americas-economic-growth/

[181] Antitrust: The Problem and Solution for Health Care," David Balto, US News and World Report, April 12, 2013: http://www.usnews.com/opinion/blogs/economic-intelligence/2013/04/12/after-affordable-care-act-new-antitrust-laws-needed-in-health-care

[182] The Justice Dept. has opened an investigation into collusion to keep prices high. "US airlines investigated over ticket prices," BBC News, Business (1 July 2015): http://www.bbc.com/news/business-33353360

[183] See "The hidden redistribution of wealth: upward," Robert Reich, Opinion, San Francisco Chronicle, Nov. 4, 2015: http://www.sfgate.com/opinion/reich/article/The-hidden-redistribution-of-wealth-upward-6611176.php

[184] "Why Falling Food Prices Around the World Aren't Helping U.S. Consumers," Jordan Yadoo, BloombergBusiness (July 16, 2015): http://www.bloomberg.com/news/articles/2015-07-16/why-falling-food-prices-around-the-world-aren-t-helping-u-s-consumers

[185] "The problem with profits," The Economist (March 26th-April 1st 2016): http://www.economist.com/news/leaders/21695392-big-firms-united-states-have-never-had-it-so-good-time-more-competition-problem

[186] "Capitalism and its discontents - Anti-capitalism is being fuelled not just by capitalism's vices but also by its virtues," The

Economist (Oct. 3, 2015):
http://www.economist.com/news/business/21669911-anti-capitalism-being-fuelled-not-just-capitalisms-vices-also-its
[187] "The onrushing wave," The Economist (Jan. 18, 2014): http://www.economist.com/news/briefing/21594264-previous-technological-innovation-has-always-delivered-more-long-run-employment-not-less "A 2013 paper by Carl Benedikt Frey and Michael Osborne, of the University of Oxford, argued that jobs are at high risk of being automated in 47% of the occupational categories into which work is customarily sorted."
[188] "How Uber And Other On-Demand Startups Can Protect Themselves From Worker Lawsuits," Koray Bulut, Forbes (Sept. 28, 2015): http://www.forbes.com/sites/beltway/2015/09/28/how-uber-and-other-on-demand-startups-can-protect-themselves-from-worker-lawsuits/#6454e66e42b3 ; see also "Does Silicon Valley Have a Contract-Worker Problem?" Kevin Roose, New York Magazine (Sept. 18, 2014): http://nymag.com/daily/intelligencer/2014/09/silicon-valleys-contract-worker-problem.html
[189] Another trend over the last 40 years has been a huge increase in both spouses working, and workers taking less vacation time. Workers took an average of 16 days of vacation in 2013 compared to an average of 20.3 days as recently as 2000. Thus, most people are working harder for the same or lesser pay, after inflation. See "Americans taking fewest vacation days in four decades," Chuck Thompson, CNN (Oct. 23, 2014): http://www.cnn.com/2014/10/22/travel/u-s-workers-vacation-time/
[190] "The League of Dangerous Mapmakers," Robert Draper, The Atlantic (October 2012): http://www.theatlantic.com/magazine/archive/2012/10/the-league-of/309084/
[191] "Indiana Becomes 6th State to Call for Article V Convention of States," Barbara Hollingsworth, cnsnews.com (March 2, 2016): http://www.cnsnews.com/news/article/barbara-hollingsworth/indiana-passes-article-v-resolution-6th-state-call-convention

[192] "Harvard Confab Fails to Convince Tea Party to Seek Constitutional Convention," Thomas R. Eddlem, New American (Sept. 25, 2011): http://www.thenewamerican.com/usnews/constitution/item/8055-harvard-confab-fails-to-convince-tea-party-to-seek-constitutional-convention

[193] https://en.wikipedia.org/wiki/Campaign_finance_reform_in_the_United_States

[194] "Types of Advocacy Groups," Opensecrets.org: https://www.opensecrets.org/527s/types.php

[195] "Overview of State Laws on Public Financing," National Conference of State Legislatures: http://www.ncsl.org/research/elections-and-campaigns/public-financing-of-campaigns-overview.aspx

[196] "FEC: $7B spent on 2012 campaign," Tarini Parti, Politico (01/31/13): http://www.politico.com/story/2013/01/7-billion-spent-on-2012-campaign-fec-says-087051

[197] "More than Combating Corruption: The Other Benefits of Public Financing," Mimi Murray Digby Marziani, Adam Skaggs, Brennan Center for Justice (Oct. 7, 2011): https://www.brennancenter.org/analysis/more-combating-corruption-other-benefits-public-financing

[198] An example of a politician who benefited from public funding is Ronald Reagan, who was otherwise virtually out of money in his 1st, unsuccessful bid for president against Gerald Ford, where he gained prominence and set up his later successful run.

[199] Note that HR 137 was introduced in the 112th Congress to require radio and television broadcasters to provide free broadcasting time for political advertising. See also http://fairelectionsnow.org/

[200] "Public Financing," League of Women Voters: http://lwv.org/tags/public-financing

[201] "Half in U.S. Support Publicly Financed Federal Campaigns," Lydia Saad, Gallup.com (June 24, 2013): http://www.gallup.com/poll/163208/half-support-publicly-financed-federal-campaigns.aspx

[202] See http://en.wikipedia.org/wiki/Redistricting_commission

[203] "Supreme Court Backs Arizona's Redistricting Commission Targeting Gridlock," Bill Chappell, KQED Public Radio (June 29, 2015): http://www.npr.org/sections/thetwo-way/2015/06/29/418521823/supreme-court-backs-arizonas-redistricting-commission-targeting-gridlock

[204] For current redistricting efforts, see http://www.americansforredistrictingreform.org

[205] For current efforts to fix the senate, see http://fixthesenatenow.org

[206] "The revolving door spins faster: Ex-Congressmen become 'stealth lobbyists,' " Michael Hiltzik, Los Angeles Times (Jan. 6, 2016): http://www.latimes.com/business/hiltzik/la-fi-mh-the-revolving-door-20150106-column.html

[207] "The 'Permanent Campaign' = Perpetual Paralysis: For starters, make House terms four years and junk the primary system," William A. Galston, Wall Street Journal, Oct. 28, 2014.

[208] "How Smart Fiscal Rules Keep Sweden's Budget in Balance," Ed Dolan, Business Insider (Aug. 1, 2011): http://www.businessinsider.com/how-smart-fiscal-rules-keep-swedens-budget-in-balance-2011-8

[209]

https://en.m.wikipedia.org/wiki/United_States_presidential_primary

[210] Eric Black also proposes a supermajority for ruling laws unconstitutional, such as a 6-3 majority. Although this sounds good in theory, with the basic gridlock potential built into our divided government, this would eliminate a needed safety value. The beauty of the Supreme Court is that they have to make decisions, they can't just punt like Congress. See Eric Black, Imperfect Union: The Constitutional Roots of the Mess We're In. See also "Some ideas to limit the 'supremacy' of the U.S. Supreme Court," Eric Black MinnPost (Nov. 27, 2012): https://www.minnpost.com/eric-black-ink/2012/11/some-ideas-limit-supremacy-us-supreme-court

[211] https://en.wikipedia.org/wiki/Base_Realignment_and_Closure

[212] "The Truth About Term Limits," Alan Greenblatt, Governing.com (January 2006): http://www.governing.com/topics/politics/Truth-Term-Limits.html. See also "Term Limits Don't Work," Stanley M. Caress, U.S. News & World Report (Jan. 16, 2015): http://www.usnews.com/opinion/articles/2015/01/16/states-show-term-limits-wouldnt-work-for-congress. For an argument in favor of term limits, see "Testimony, Congressional Term Limits," Edward H. Crane, Subcommittee on the Constitution, Committee on the Judiciary, United States Senate (January 25, 1995): http://www.cato.org/publications/congressional-testimony/congressional-term-limits

[213] *U.S. Term Limits, Inc. v. Thornton*, 514 U.S. 779 (1995).

[214] "A simple way to fix gridlock in Congress -- change committees," Brian Feinstein, LA Times (Jan. 4, 2015): http://www.latimes.com/opinion/op-ed/la-oe-feinstein-congress-committees-random-assignment-20150105-story.html

[215] See endnotes under the section "Changes that crippled compromise." Also, the Hewlett Foundation initiated the Madison Initiative in 2014 to come up with ways to encourage compromise in Congress, with the report due to its Board in 2017: http://hewlett.org/programs/special-projects/madison-initiative

[216] "Policy Basics: Where Do Our Federal Tax Dollars Go?" Center on Budget and Policy Priorities (updated March 4, 2016): http://www.cbpp.org/cms/?fa=view&id=1258

[217] "Defense contractors spend millions lobbying Congress, get billions in new budget," Eric Boehm, Watchdog.org (January 22, 2014): http://watchdog.org/124909/defense-spending/

[218] "Top 10 Tax Breaks that May Be Eliminated," Eric Pianin, The Fiscal Times (Sept. 13, 2012): http://www.thefiscaltimes.com/Articles/2012/09/13/Top-10-Tax-Breaks-that-May-Be-Elimated

[219] "Report: The Big Money in Tax Breaks Continues," Becky Sweger, National Priorities Project (April 18, 2014):

http://nationalpriorities.org/analysis/2014/big-money-tax-breaks/exposing-big-money-tax-breaks/
[220] "The Tax Break-Down: Preferential Rates on Capital Gains," Committee for a Responsible Federal Budget (Aug. 27, 2013): http://crfb.org/blogs/tax-break-down-preferential-rates-capital-gains
[221] "A New Look At How We All Benefit From Tax Breaks," Howard Gleckman, Forbes (Dec. 19, 2013: http://www.forbes.com/sites/beltway/2013/12/19/a-new-look-at-how-we-all-benefit-from-tax-breaks/#386bdfd35927
[222] "Offshore Tax Havens Cost Average Taxpayer $1,259 a Year, Small Businesses $3,923," Dan Smith, U.S. PIRG The Federation of State PIRGS (April 15, 2014): http://www.uspirg.org/news/usp/offshore-tax-havens-cost-average-taxpayer-1259-year-small-businesses-3923
[223] "Corporate Welfare in the Federal Budget," Tad DeHaven, Cato Institute (July 25, 2012): http://www.cato.org/publications/policy-analysis/corporate-welfare-federal-budget
[224] "The Estate Tax Is a Huge Giveaway in the Fiscal-Cliff Talks," Matthew O'Brien, The Atlantic (Dec. 31, 2012): http://www.theatlantic.com/business/archive/2012/12/the-estate-tax-is-a-huge-giveaway-in-the-fiscal-cliff-talks/266723/
[225] "IRS Funding Cuts Are Costly for Taxpayers and the Budget," Nathaniel Frentz, Center on Budget and Policy Priorities (Feb. 20, 2014): http://www.offthechartsblog.org/irs-funding-cuts-are-costly-for-taxpayers-and-the-budget/
[226] Taxpayers for Common Sense: Summary of Senate Finance Committee's Tax Extenders Package, April 3. 2014: http://www.taxpayer.net/library/article/summary-of-tax-extenders
[227] "America's Most Obvious Tax Reform Idea: Kill the Oil and Gas Subsidies," Jordan Weissmann, The Atlantic (March 19, 2013): http://www.theatlantic.com/business/archive/2013/03/americas-most-obvious-tax-reform-idea-kill-the-oil-and-gas-subsidies/274121/

[228] "Taxpayers Turn U.S. Farmers Into Fat Cats With Subsidies," David J. Lynch and Alan Bjerga, Bloomberg (Sept. 9, 2013): http://www.bloomberg.com/news/2013-09-09/farmers-boost-revenue-sowing-subsidies-for-crop-insurance.html
[229] "Here's Everything You've Always Wanted To Know About Lobbying For Your Business," Steven Strauss, Business Insider (Nov. 25, 2011): http://www.businessinsider.com/everything-you-always-wanted-to-know-about-lobbying-2011-11
[230] "Remember That $83 Billion Bank Subsidy? We Weren't Kidding," Editorial Board, BloombergView (Feb. 24, 2013): http://www.bloombergview.com/articles/2013-02-24/remember-that-83-billion-bank-subsidy-we-weren-t-kidding
[231] "With Lobbying Blitz, For-Profit Colleges Diluted New Rules," Eric Lichtblau, Common Dreams (Dec. 10, 2011): http://www.commondreams.org/news/2011/12/10/lobbying-blitz-profit-colleges-diluted-new-rules
[232] "Myth 21: Carseats are safer than seatbelts for ages 2+," Angeline Duran Piotrowski, Mommy My6th Buster (Nov. 23, 2008): http://mommymythbuster.wordpress.com/2008/11/23/myth-21-carseats-are-safer-than-seatbelts-for-2-and-over/ See also: "The Seat-Belt Solution," Stephen J. Dubner and Steven D. Levitt, The New York Times (July 10, 2005): http://pricetheory.uchicago.edu/levitt/Papers/SeatBeltSolution.pdf
[233] How Government Unions Are Destroying California, Bob Loewen, Unionwatch.org (January 26, 2016): http://unionwatch.org/how-government-unions-are-destroying-california-2/

CPSIA information can be obtained
at www.ICGtesting.com
Printed in the USA
FSOW04n1823041116
26876FS